Peacock, Alan T., 19/The economic theory
HJ135 .P4 1976 B C.1 STACKS 1976

HJ 135 P4 1976b Peacock, Alan T., 1922—
The economic theory of fiscal policy

HJ 135 P4 1976b Peacock, Alan T., 1922—
The economic theory of fiscal policy

DATE	ISSUED TO

COLLEGE FOR HUMAN SERVICES
LIBRARY
345 HUDSON STREET
NEW YORK, N.Y. 10014

The Economic Theory of Fiscal Policy

by
Alan Peacock
Professor of Economics, University of York

and

G. K. Shaw
Reader in Economics, University of St. Andrews

Second Edition

ST. MARTIN'S PRESS   NEW YORK

© *George Allen and Unwin (Publishers) Ltd, 1971 and 1976*

All rights reserved. For information, write:
St. Martin's Press, Inc., 175 Fifth Avenue, New York, N.Y. 10010

Printed in Great Britain

Library of Congress Catalog Card Number: 76–15870
Second Edition first published in the United States of America in 1976

FIRST EDITION PUBLISHED IN 1971

CONTENTS

	Page
PREFACE TO THE FIRST EDITION	5
PREFACE TO THE SECOND EDITION	7

PART ONE: THE MACROECONOMIC ANALYSIS OF FISCAL POLICY

I	The Scope of the Work	11
II	The Static Theory of Fiscal Policy: Closed Economy	24
III	The Static Theory of Fiscal Policy: Open Economy	44
IV	Fiscal Policy, Employment and the Price Level	66
V	Fiscal Policy and Economic Growth	80
VI	Stabilization Policy in a Dynamic Setting	99
	Appendix to Part One: A Simple Non-linear Model of Fiscal Policy	120

PART TWO: FISCAL POLICY AND THE THEORY OF ECONOMIC POLICY

VII	Policy Targets and Fiscal Instruments	127
VIII	Fiscal Policy and Constrained Maximization	137
IX	Fiscal Policy and Uncertainty: an Introduction	160
	Appendix A: Suggestions for Additional Reading	178
	Appendix B: The Main Symbols Used	184
INDEX OF NAMES		189
INDEX OF SUBJECTS		191

PREFACE TO THE FIRST EDITION

This book seeks to answer the question what can economic analysis tell us about the effects of various fiscal measures on the value of those macroeconomic variables whose movements are taken as a guide to the performance of the economy, e.g. income, output, employment, growth, prices and the balance of payments. Its point of departure is the conventional macroeconomic model, embodying government taxation and expenditure, which still dominates even fairly advanced textbooks in economics and is the implicit model in much of the popular journalistic discussion of fiscal policy. The shortcomings of the conventional model have been clearly recognized in the growing economics literature associated with the theory of economic policy. Briefly put, these shortcomings are the association of the problem of maintaining stability with only one important economic variable, the level of money income, and the *simpliste* nature of the economic system which is embodied in the model.

A fair proportion of the professional literature on the theory of economic policy employs very sophisticated tools of analysis, and this accounts for the difficulty of translating it into terms more familiar to the economist specializing in public finance. In seeking to answer the general question referred to, we have used simpler mathematical techniques, while still conveying, so it is hoped, the important improvements in the formulation of the analysis of policy problems which the theory of economic policy has provided.

Fortunately, it is now common practice in reputable universities to insist that undergraduates specializing in economics must be able to understand mathematical models and to discern their relevance in the formulation of policy problems. It is a sign of the revolution in economics education that we can state with some confidence that a student who has grasped the elements of mathematical economics should have no difficulty in following this text. Therefore, we hope that it will be a useful addition to the literature recommended for macroeconomics courses from the intermediate level upwards, and for public finance courses for undergraduates and graduate students in which the economics of fiscal policy plays a substantial role. At the same time, we believe that economists closely involved in research and policy-making in government and business may find it useful to consult a work which offers a conspectus of recent academic thinking on matters which are their day-to-day concern. This belief rests on more than faith in the need for a constant dialogue between theorist and practitioner, but upon our own occasional employment as consultants to governments and international organizations. Indeed, the choice of illustrations of the use of particular models have been influenced considerably by the investigations we have been asked to undertake for such bodies.

Some of the text of this volume reworks previous contributions by the authors to professional journals. Acknowledgement is made to these sources at the appropriate place, but in a few instances we have left the original text unchanged. Various of our academic colleagues have been persuaded to comment on particular sections of the work. We would like to thank in particular Mr Michael Jones-Lee for a barrage of suggestions and criticisms. For permission to use hitherto unpublished material we are especially indebted to Professor Robert W. Kilpatrick of Cornell University. We are most grateful to both the Department of Economics and the Institute of Social and Economic Research for typing assistance, and hope that Miss Mary Robinson and Mrs Susan Loft of these institutions respectively will acquire no long-standing aversion to the Greek alphabet in the course of their much appreciated labours. Finally, Alan Peacock would like to record his warm appreciation for the use of the facilities of the Fondazione Luigi Einaudi, Turin, Italy, where, as a visiting research professor, he was able to complete some necessary revisions to part of the manuscript.

A.P.
G.K.S.

PREFACE TO THE SECOND EDITION

The opportunity to publish a second edition of this work has enabled the authors to make a number of corrections and some substantial alterations which we hope add up to an improvement in the original. The main alterations are as follows:

Firstly, there has been a very thorough revision of Part I of the work in order to demonstrate more explicitly the influence of recent developments in macroeconomic theory on the assessment of the effects of budgetary transactions on the economy. Chapter III in particular has been practically rewritten to take more account of monetarist arguments which can be assimilated in the extended Keynesian system and which are therefore capable of expression in standard macroeconomic terminology.

Secondly, it seemed to us that Chapter IV of the original edition, whilst usefully spelling out the modifications following from disaggregation, offered some fairly obvious conclusions and could be dispensed with, and that a necessary extension of the theory was more important than a superficial account of the econometrics of fiscal policy as contained in the original Chapter X: From Theory to Practice. In place of this final chapter, a wholly new chapter introducing recent discussion of the conduct of fiscal policy under conditions of uncertainty seemed more useful for the reader.

Thirdly, close scrutiny by friends and critics, and particularly by vigilant translators of the work into Italian, Japanese and Spanish, revealed, alongside our own painful discoveries, a number of annoying errors in the transcription of equations and a few mathematical slips. Hopefully we have managed to eradicate these.

In addition to those whose help in preparing the first edition has already been acknowledged with gratitude, we should like to add the names of Professor T. Nosse of the Kobe University of Commerce, Mr Stokes, Assistant Professor, University of Groningen, and Professor Abello of the University of Barcelona, who supplied us with a list of suggested corrections, and also Mr John Hey of the University of York for reading and commenting on the revised final chapter.

PART ONE

THE MACROECONOMIC ANALYSIS OF FISCAL POLICY

Chapter I

THE SCOPE OF THE WORK

I. INTRODUCTION

The purpose of this work is to offer a review of the economics of fiscal policy which takes account of some major post-Keynesian developments in macroeconomic theory.[1] While both the theory and the public finance measures which influence the economy will have been studied by those likely to read this volume, the authors have been struck by the paucity of attempts to bring them both together. On the one hand, macroeconomic models, which have undergone rapid transformation in the hands of such writers as Harrod, Hicks, Samuelson, Solow, Kaldor, Kalecki and Domar, rarely specify the transactions of the system of public finance in sufficient detail in order to understand their influence on the economy. On the other hand, writers of public finance text-books have employed models of the economy in studying, for example, the possibility of achieving economic stability by budgetary means, which can only be described as *simpliste*. There are notable exceptions to this criticism,[2] but at the time of writing the attempts at marrying the recent analytical developments in macroeconomics and the influence of the system of public finance on the economy are still largely buried in the covers of professional academic journals.

In order to explain how the attempt is made to bridge the gap between the innovations in economic analytics and their application to the study of fiscal policy, it is necessary to say something about some recent developments in economic theory. The rest of this introductory chapter discusses some of these developments and in so doing offers a rationale for the scope and content of this work.

II. THE KEYNESIAN ANALYSIS OF FISCAL POLICY

A fairly standard treatment of the economic theory of fiscal policy in text-books on public finance may be caricatured in the following way. A 'target' national income (= expenditure) is chosen as being consistent with the objective of 'full employment' (of labour). This target is a unique value of a dependent variable, national income, which is influenced by several exogeneously determined variables some of which are assumed to be under government control. The government, through the system of public finance, is made to influence the size of the national expenditure, usually in two ways. Government expenditure on goods and services is itself a component of national expenditure. Variations in government revenue, usually represented only by a proportional tax on personal income, can affect the level of consumer expenditure on goods and services, which is usually the major component (in size) of national expenditure. All that the government need do in order to stabilize the economy at the 'target' level of income (and therefore employment) is to alter the proportional income tax rate or the size of government expenditure, the amount of the alteration depending on the value of the Keynesian multiplier. A breath of realism can be introduced into the analysis by placing certain constraints on government action, such as the requirement that politicians do not like unbalanced budgets. It can then be shown that achieving the desired target is still possible, but requires larger changes in government expenditure and income, because of the (assumed) smaller multiplier effect of a balanced budget. Or, it may be assumed that both tax rates and expenditure rates are difficult to change in the short run, and simple economic analysis is used to show that all is not lost, because some taxes and transfer payments (e.g. unemployment benefits) are automatic stabilizers.

This caricature is only a means of directing attention to the salient features of common text-book presentation, and allowance must be made for the fact that even within the narrow scope offered by the simple model of income determination, many variations in exposition and in content are possible. Also, it may be argued, as, indeed we accept in Chapter II, that the simple Keynesian theory of income determination is a reasonable point of departure for the study of fiscal policy designed to achieve economic stability. However, it is little more than this.

If we wish to develop a model which may offer a framework for policy-making, we must go much further, as an examination of the omissions from the simple analysis will indicate.

III. EXTENDING AND MODIFYING THE SIMPLE KEYNESIAN MODEL

Let it be assumed for the moment that the main interest of the model lies in examining the effects of the budget on the level of national income. The model may be said to be incomplete in the sense that there are other influences on the level of national income which either influence that level directly or through the independent variables, consumption, investment, already identified. The most obvious example is the neglect in the basic Keynesian equation of income determination of the influence of the monetary system. As Chapter II indicates, even simple assumptions, such as the exogenous determination of the money supply, the determination of the rate of interest by money supply and the level of national income, and the dependence of the level of investment on the rate of interest, offer substantial modifications to the simplified analysis. It is to be noted that these modifications are carried out within the 'standard' Keynesian framework, which assumes that changes in the supply of money affect the level of income only via changes in the rate of interest and hence in the level of investment. One does not need to invoke neo-classical monetary theory which would have us regard the level of *consumption* as a function of changes in the quantity of money. [3]

One important corollary of the introduction of the monetary system is that, in estimating the effects of fiscal policy on the level of income, we have to specify clearly the assumptions being made about monetary policy. It must also be noted in passing that budget changes themselves, in so far as these result in government surpluses and deficits, may affect the supply of money depending on whether surpluses draw cash from and deficits push cash into the economic system.

The introduction of the monetary system does not extend the number of terms in the basic income equation $Y = C + I + G$, but makes it unnecessary for I to be treated as an autonomous variable in order to solve for Y, i.e. by making I dependent on the rate of interest, and the rate of interest dependent on the supply of money as well as the level of income. A more obvious indication of the deficiencies of the simple Keynesian fiscal policy model is to be found in the assumption of a closed economy. Chapter III of this volume examines what happens when this assumption is removed and the income equation is extended to include the balance of payments. Controlling the level of Y by taxes and government expenditure becomes, therefore, a complex matter, when the level of income itself depends on transactions with other countries. It becomes even more complex when fiscal policy has to take account not only of the degree of 'openness' of the economy but also of the effects of monetary policy on the balance of payments, in judging the correct adjustments to be made in achieving the 'target' level of income.

It was early realized in the development of modern macroeconomic theory that the relation between changes in investment and consumption and changes in income were not independent of the degree of aggregation of economic transactions. This point has often been illustrated by dividing consumers into 'workers' and 'capitalists', the former having a marginal propensity to consume of unity and the latter a marginal propensity to consume of less than unity. A redistribution of income brought about by fiscal means, e.g. by the differential impact of taxes and/or transfer payments, between workers and capitalists would therefore alter the aggregated marginal propensity to consume and, consequently, the level of national income. If it were desired to raise the level of national income, this could be done by making the distribution of disposable income (factor income + transfers—taxes) more equal and vice versa if policy demanded a lowering of the level of national income. Many variations can be developed on the theme of disaggregation, including such interesting cases (from the policy point of view) as the disaggregation of government expenditure by type of purchase, and the disaggregation of budget transactions by layer of government. These forms of disaggregation are not explored in this edition.

IV. THE 'TARGET VARIABLE' AMBIGUITY

So far, we have shown how the Keynesian-type model needs modification in order to take account of the structure of actual economic systems, but throughout the process of modification it has invariably been assumed that the basic purpose of the analysis is to determine the effects of fiscal policy on the level of national income, the target variable.

The concentration of interest on this target variable arose from the association of fluctuations in employment of labour with fluctuations in income. Given the widespread acceptance of the need for full employment of labour, it is a simple step to assume that the task of fiscal policy is to stabilize national income at a level compatible with this objective. The function $N = N(Y)$, where N is the number of employed persons, and Y, money national income, clearly telescopes a chain of reasoning which begins at one end with the proposition that $N = N(Q, w)$, where Q is national output and w 'the' wage rate, and $Q = Q(Y)$, i.e. output is a function of the level of aggregate demand or money national income.

As is well known, Keynes was one of the first to recognize that increases in aggregate demand in conditions where all resources are fully employed, will result in the short run in an increase in the general price level and not in an increase in employment.

The general acceptance of avoidance of inflation leads to the first important dichotomy in the objective function denoting economic stability into 'full employment of labour' and 'price stability'.

In order to cope with the problem of associating changes in employment with changes in output, Keynesian models have been squared with the traditional marginal productivity theory of factor inputs by assuming: (a) that the marginal = average productivity of labour; (b) that up to the full employment level, 'the' wage rate is constant; and (c) that in the short run an increase in investment only affects the level of demand and not the level of output. These assumptions make it possible to assume that the aggregate supply curve is horizontal up to the full employment level, and that employment is a linear function of aggregate supply (output). Beyond the full employment point, the aggregate supply function has an elasticity of zero and any increase in aggregate demands results in a proportional increase in the general price level. [4]

The result of these subterfuges in assumption-making appears to have been designed to hold to the proposition that fiscal policy still need only keep national income at that unique level at which full employment is achieved and inflation is just about to begin. However, we cannot be content to accept this 'let-out', even although, as Chapter IV indicates, the adoption of more realistic assumptions leads to analytical complications. We must take account of recent empirical research which denies that full employment, as a political objective, is compatible with stable prices. We must also take into account the fact that the tax system impinges on the economy not solely in the form of taxes on incomes but also in the form of taxes on goods and services. These latter—consumption taxes are an obvious example—require us to look more closely at the reactions of producers to tax changes, and how these are reflected in their pricing decisions and in their demand for labour.

V. THE SHORT PERIOD AND THE LONG PERIOD

So far we have examined quite a number of ways in which the simple Keynesian model must be modified in order to define the task of fiscal policy, given the single objective of maintaining full employment without inflation. As yet, the model in all its variants deals only with the short run, during which period of time the labour force is constant in size, and changes in the capital stock reflected in alterations in I affect only the level of money national income and not the level of (potential) national output. In the longer run, it is manifest that neither of these assumptions will hold.

It is not necessary to describe in any detail how the Keynesian short-period model has been transformed into the Harrod—Domar type growth model, for the process is familiar even to first-year economics students.[5] Preserving economic stability, in the sense of maintaining full employment without inflation, now requires the adjustment of aggregate demand to a growth *path* of output and employment and not to a unique level of national income. The interesting problem encountered in using fiscal weapons for this purpose is that one has to bear in mind that tax and expenditure changes may not only affect the level of aggregate demand, but also the growth path itself. An obvious example is an increase in government expenditure on education which, *ceteris paribus*, increases aggregate demand, but at the same time, adds to the stock of capital and is therefore likely to increase potential output through the improvement in skills.

Chapter V follows standard practice in demonstrating how budgetary transactions can be introduced into the simple Harrod—Domar growth model, but the model itself includes an explicit functional relationship not between output and employment but only between output and the growth in the capital stock. One way round this difficulty is to assume that labour and capital are employed in fixed proportions. This means that the task of the fiscal system becomes the rather complicated one of marrying the growth in capital stock to the growth in the labour force and ensuring that aggregate demand is just sufficient to absorb the resultant output.

However, it is now widely accepted in economics that the assumption of fixed proportions is an extreme one and that it is more reasonable to assume that elasticity of substitution between capital and labour is positive. Recent discussion of growth theory has been largely dominated by the use of models which postulate constant returns to scale and an elasticity of substitution between capital and labour of unity, as in the simple version of the Cobb-Douglas Function.[6] Such models demonstrate that the economy automatically adjusts to the long-run growth in the labour force, thus, apparently, making fiscal adjustments designed to achieve full employment unnecessary. Chapter V shows that this extreme conclusion assumes that the community is indifferent to the speed of adjustment to the equilibrium growth level which produces full employment and also that technical progress is ignored. We are able to show that fiscal policy still has a role to play, when these factors are brought into reckoning.

One further important point about the study of the long period is that it concentrates attention on other policy objectives of interest to the community, such as provision of a 'satisfactory' rate of growth in income and/or consumption per head, alongside a 'satisfactory' employment level. We shall show later that the move away from the traditional Keynesian 'one-target' model to a 'multi-target' one offers the opportunity of integrating the analysis of fiscal policy with what is now termed the theory of economic policy. All that need be said here is that we shall show that the Keynesian analysis of fiscal policy emerges as a special case within the theory of economic policy in which there is only *one* objective and *one* policy instrument, whereas in any policy situation we encounter several objectives and several policy instruments. (Cf. Section VII below.)

VI. TIME AND ECONOMIC STABILITY

The theory of income determination is usually carried out in the form of an exercise in 'comparative statics'. An equilibrium level of national income is postulated, a change takes place in one of the independent variables, and 'hey presto' a new level of national income is determined. It is clear that any such adjustment from one level of income to another must take time, so the analysis either is being totally unrealistic by assuming instantaneous adjustment, or incomplete in not specifying the time path. It is also implicit that, in the process of adjustment, no further disturbances take place after the initial change in one of the independent variables, or simultaneous initial change in more than one.

Time more clearly enters the picture in growth models, for changes in the size of working population and capital stock and resultant changes in the flow of output postulate a time continuum. Nevertheless, the use of any policy instrument, such as a change in tax rates, is completely independent of the time period of adjustment. For example, if the growth rate requires to be raised, say by raising the annual rate of investment, a change in one of the fiscal parameters to achieve this end is immediately reflected in a change in the growth rate.

One of the earliest and most fruitful modifications of the Keynesian comparative static model was designed to explain the observed phenomenon of cyclical movements through time in income and employment. The famous Samuelson combination of the multiplier and the accelerator, which traced out such fluctuations, given that the consumption coefficient and accelerator assumed values within a certain range, was able to arrive at this result by the plausible assumption of lagged adjustment. Thus, consumption was made a lagged function of income and investment a lagged function of the rate of change in consumption (or in later formulations, income). It is rather surprising that the reformulation of the income equation as a second-order difference equation did not embrace fiscal variables at a much earlier stage than occurred. The Samuelson equation appeared in 1939, the equation plus fiscal variables not until 1961. What we are able to show (Chapter VI), building on recent analysis, is that both discretionary and automatic changes in fiscal policy can in some circumstances be de-stabilizing, as a consequence of the lagged responses of fiscal changes, to changes in the level of national income. Similarly, we can show that automatic changes in tax yields without changes in tax rates can result in aggregate demands falling below what is required to maintain stable growth, as compared with the common conclusion in the static Keynesian model that the built-in stability resulting from the tax system can never fully compensate for any autonomous shift in one of the independent variables which results in a rise (fall) in income.

VII. THE 'TRADE-OFF' PROBLEM

As already mentioned, the simple type of analysis of fiscal policy asks the questions: 'What determines the level of national income?' and 'How can the level of national income be influenced by fiscal means in order to achieve economic stability?' We have, so far, concentrated largely on the procedures which must be followed in developing satisfactory models which seek to answer the first of these questions. It is now time to consider in more detail the content of the second.

Perhaps the best way of considering the second question is to list the macroeconomic variables which are associated with economic stability. Those singled out for special consideration are the level of employment, the general level of prices, and exports and imports (the balance of payments). Thus it is commonly accepted that values of these variables must be attained which ensure full employment of labour, a stable (or gently rising) price level and 'equilibrium' in the balance of payments, i.e. no deficits in the balance of payments with a fixed exchange rate. The simultaneous achievement of all these elements of economic stability, as is plain from recent economic history, is difficult enough to attain, but stability does not exhaust the list of policy objectives whose fulfilment is supposed to be influenced by the fiscal system. In Section V above, we mentioned recent interest in the growth performance of the economy, and one might add in a 'satisfactory' distribution of income and even wealth. It would be pure chance, therefore, if some specific value of Y would represent a bliss point at which all these objectives would be simultaneously reached.

We also saw earlier (Section III) that the effectiveness of fiscal policy depends on what assumptions are made about the monetary system and how monetary policy is assumed to operate. In short, we have to know something about the degree of *co-ordination* in the use of policy instruments. Likewise, the effectiveness of any given fiscal policy depends upon the *choice of objectives*, and the relative weight assigned to each one. In the language of the economic pundits, we have to specify the community's 'social welfare (or objective) function'.

It is for this reason that we have turned in the latter part of this volume to consider the place of fiscal policy within the framework of the theory of economic policy, associated particularly with the Dutch economists, Tinbergen and Theil.[7] Briefly put, what the theory of economic policy does is to explore the analogy between the maximization of utility by an individual economic unit (consumer, producer) subject to constraints and by the government as the body responsible for meeting the community's desired objectives. Policy targets are specified, such as those listed above, and are embodied in a community objective function. These are the dependent variables in the relevant economic model. Policy instruments are then specified, and these are reflected in the independent variables in the economic model. The essential problem which the theory of economic policy tries to solve is that of devising a feasible combination of targets and instruments, subject to the constraints presented by the structure of the economy. The structure of the economy is, of course, represented by the system of equations which embody the economic model. (For further discussion, see Chapters VII and VIII.) Within this framework, we can examine how far fiscal policy is the appropriate instrument among the set of instruments available to the government to achieve any particular target or set of targets.

It may be useful to offer a diagrammatic representation of the methodology of the theory of economic policy, but with special reference to the role of fiscal policy (see Figure I.1). In this Figure, social welfare is a function of two objectives: (a) the 'desired' rate of growth, Y^r, defined as the rate of increase in real output, Y; and (b) economic stability, i.e. *ex ante* saving, S_x, and investment, I_x, have to be equal at the full employment of resources level. These two policy objectives may be influenced via the effect on the economic system as described in the

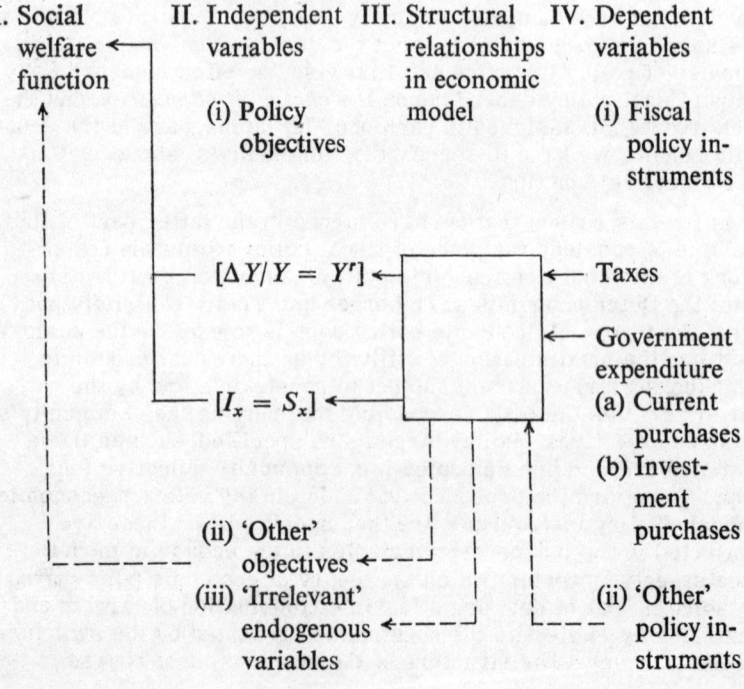

Figure I.1 Schema of Theory of Fiscal Policy.

model by fiscal policy instruments. The hatched lines merely denote that, in other contexts, other objectives and other policy instruments may be relevant.

One point worth noting in passing is that we have assumed that the social welfare function is maximized by achieving the *target* rate of growth and the equality of savings and investment, *ex ante*. There is no necessary reason why, subject to the constraints of the model, it should be possible to achieve these two objectives simultaneously by fiscal policy, or by fiscal policy in combination with other policy instruments. The analogy here is with a situation in which a consumer has a limited income but wishes to consume specific amounts of a range of commodities which, at given prices, would more than exhaust the income available. To reach the optimal position consistent with limited income, the consumer must decide, in the light of his preference system, what amounts of which commodities he will be prepared to give up. There is no particular reason why he should just give up consuming one commodity altogether.

Similarly, if both the community targets cannot be achieved simultaneously, there is no particular reason why the 'next best' position is to achieve one at the expense of the other. The 'next best' situation may be one in which, for example, the community may prefer a slightly lower rate of growth and full employment with some rise in prices, rather than full employment without inflation and an even lower rate of growth. In other words, we must specify the preference function of the community which depicts the 'trade-off' between growth and stability. This is the essential difference between the Tinbergen approach, which concentrates on target values of policy objectives, and the Theil approach, which explores the possibility of 'trade-off'.

VIII. THE MATHEMATICAL CONTENT OF THIS VOLUME

One of the main attractions of simple macroeconomic models lies in the fact that they can be expressed in very simple linear algebra. Taking account of the extensions of these models which are necessary for our purpose means that this volume must embrace a much wider and somewhat more difficult mathematical analysis. So far as possible, we have tried in this volume to proceed from the simpler mathematics to the more complex forms alongside the development from the simple Keynesian models to their more realistic counterparts. The standard of mathematics presupposed is no more than that commonly expected of students specializing in economics at the undergraduate level.[8]

One complication resulting from the extension of the mathematical analysis of fiscal policy is that more symbols must be used. So far as possible, we have tried to assign the common definition to a symbol used in economic analysis, and to economize in the use of symbols by the use of superscripts and subscripts. For example, Y is defined as Gross National Product in real terms, Y^m = Gross National Product or Income in money terms, Y^r = the 'required' or equilibrium growth of GNP, Y^d = disposable income, Y^d_b = disposable income of country B, and so on. Capital Arabic letters, so far as possible, are used for aggregates, lower case Greek letters for constants and lower case Arabic letters for coefficients, functional relationships and ratios. The reader must face the fact, however, that in order to provide a consistent definition of a symbol throughout the book, consistency must be traded off against proliferation of symbols. In order to assist the reader, a comprehensive list of symbols and their definitions together with an explanation of their use is given at the end of the volume.

NOTES

(1) For a comprehensive review of the theory, see R. G. D. Allen, *Macro-Economic Theory*, Macmillan, London, 1968.

(2) Such as Bent Hansen, *The Economic Theory of Fiscal Policy*, Allen & Unwin, London, 1958; R. A. Musgrave, *The Theory of Public Finance*, McGraw-Hill, New York, 1959; L. Johansen, *Public Economics*, North Holland Publishing Co., Amsterdam, 1965; and Carl Shoup, *Public Finance*, Aldine Press, Chicago, 1969.

(3) For a clear and relatively simple exposition of classical macroeconomics, see Gardner Ackley, *Macroeconomic Theory*, Macmillan, New York, 1961. For a more specific analysis of monetary theory and consumption see Don Patinkin, *Money, Interest and Prices*, 2nd edn., Harper International edition, New York, 1966.

(4) See, for example, Martin Bronfenbrenner and Frank D. Holzmann, 'A Survey of Inflation Theory', *Surveys of Economic Theory*, Vol. I, 1965.

(5) Cf. a well-known text such as D. M. McDougall and T. E. Dernberg, *Macroeconomics*, Student International edition, McGraw-Hill, New York, 1963, Ch. 16.

(6) For an excellent exposition of neo-classical growth theory, see F. H. Hahn and R. C. O. Matthews, 'The Theory of Economic Growth: A Survey', *Surveys of Economic Theory*, Vol. II, 1965.

(7) See Jan Tinbergen, 'On the Theory of Economic Policy', *Contributions to Economic Analysis*, 2nd edn., Vol. I, North Holland Publishing Co., Amsterdam, 1952, and Henri Theil, 'Economic Forecasts and Policy', *Contributions to Economic Analysis*, 2nd edn, Vol. XV, North Holland Publishing Co., Amsterdam, 1961. For an early attempt to integrate the theory of fiscal policy with the theory of economic policy, see Bent Hansen, op. cit., Ch. 1 and 2.

(8) The student will learn all the mathematics he needs from G. C. Archibald and Richard G. Lipsey, *An Introduction to a Mathematical Treatment of Economics*, 2nd edn, Weidenfeld and Nicolson, London, 1973.

Chapter II

THE STATIC THEORY OF FISCAL POLICY: CLOSED ECONOMY

I. INTRODUCTION

In the present chapter we will review familiar concepts of national income determination and then extend the analysis to consider the implications for government tax and expenditure programmes. Throughout, we will maintain the assumption of a closed economy— an important qualification which does not, however, preclude the possibility of reaching meaningful policy conclusions. This restrictive assumption will be dispensed with in Chapter III. For this initial first step into fiscal policy we will find that we need no more technique than elementary linear algebra and simple differentiation.

II. SIMPLE NATIONAL INCOME MODELS

The simplest model of national income determination is the Keynesian case which assumes a closed economy and postulates the absence of a government sector. At first glance, the assumption of no government may appear a drastic simplification until it is remembered that government purchases may conceptually be classified into either consumption or investment spending. The more serious objection to the usefulness of the model lies in the express assumption of no external sector, for it at once removes a major constraint—the possibility of a balance of payments deficit—upon domestic economic policy-making. Such an assumption is often defended as being applicable to a country with only a small international trading sector, or in the more general case to countries where exports and imports maintain a fairly rough balance over time. However, neither situation provides an adequate justification. The comparative size of the external sector in no way provides an index of its importance in constraining domestic policy as the recent experience of the United States indicates, whilst to postulate a model with exports and imports in balance is to expressly ignore the significance of the capital account. The only justification for ignoring the external sector is purely a pedagogical one; it is a useful first step towards the development of a comprehensive model which allows of both exports and imports and also the movement of capital in response to differing monetary conditions between countries.

Given such a model, our national income identity may accordingly be written as $Y \equiv C + I$, where the symbols represent national income, consumption and investment respectively. We shall assume that consumption is a linear function of national income so that $C = \alpha + bY$ where α is the amount consumed at zero income and b is the marginal propensity to consume. We now have two equations and three unknowns; to render the system determinate we adopt the Keynesian simplifying assumption that investment expenditures are autonomously determined so that $I = \bar{I}$. We now have our national income model: [1]

$$Y = C + I$$
$$C = \alpha + bY$$
$$I = \bar{I}$$

which yields the familiar solution for the equilibrium level of national income

$$Y = \frac{\alpha + \bar{I}}{1 - b} \qquad (\text{II.1})$$

Three observations are in order at this point. Firstly, whatever values are selected for α, I and b, the resulting equilibrium level of national income will always be such as to generate savings equal to the volume of investment. Within this simple framework, without a governmental or external trade sector, savings are definitionally identical to investment spending. Secondly, it will be noted that the equilibrium level of national income is only meaningful if b is less than one. A marginal propensity to consume equal to one renders the income level indeterminate; a marginal propensity in excess of one achieves the even more absurd result that the income level becomes negative. Keynes's 'great psychological law', that when income increases consumption increases but not by as much as the increase in income, is not just an acute observation of human behaviour; it is also an essential assumption required by the theory. Finally, we should emphasize that variations in Y are to be considered as indicative of changes in the level of aggregate demand and, hence, of real or monetary output and employment. Thus, implicitly, we shall assume that employment is related to the income level by a production function in the form of

$$Y = Y(N)$$

where N denotes units of employment. We adopt the traditional assumptions that

$$dY/dN > 0$$

which gives the marginal product of labour, and further we assume

$$d^2Y/dN^2 < 0$$

which corresponds to the classical assumption of diminishing returns. The production function is admittedly deficient to the extent that it ignores the influence of capital. Nonetheless, it is a convenient simplification and for present purposes it is sufficient for us to assume that an expansion of national income implies an increase in employment and vice versa. The model is a highly simplified one and its limitations and shortcomings as a guide to practical decision making are numerous. For our purposes it is sufficient to note that since it excludes not only government spending but government taxing as well it is not directly applicable to fiscal policy as such. Nonetheless, it is useful to examine some of the characteristics in somewhat more detail. The first thing to note is the various multipliers that one can extract from such a simple statement. The investment multiplier, for an autonomous change in investment spending is of course given by $dY/dI = 1/(1 - b)$. This is identical to the consumption multiplier for an autonomous change in consumption at zero income level. With respect to the level of national income, it is immaterial whether a given change occurs in α or I; in terms of the familiar national income diagram both would lead to the same raising of the combined $C + I$ schedule.[2] Thus

$$\frac{dY}{d\bar{I}} = \frac{dY}{d\alpha} = \frac{1}{1-b}$$

However, the consumption multiplier for an autonomous change in the *marginal* propensity to consume is given by

$$\frac{dY}{db} = \frac{\alpha + \bar{I}}{(1-b)^2}$$

The Static Theory of Fiscal Policy: Closed Economy

Now this distinction between the two consumption multipliers is clearly of some significance, for without invoking the Ricardian expedient of numerical examples it is fairly clear that a comparatively small change in α will have but a limited impact upon the level of national income whereas a comparatively small change in b may have a decisive impact. Normally, government policy does not consciously seek to change the marginal propensity to consume.[3] Rather, it attempts to influence the level of demand by changing the level of disposable income—that is, by provoking a movement *along* a given consumption function. However, the motives of consumer behaviour are still imperfectly understood. It may well be that government action may inadvertently influence marginal propensities—thus changing the *slope* of the consumption function and either countering or reinforcing the intended government policy. We will take up this concern with marginal propensities at a later stage when we allow for the external sector, for then we will show that a change in the direction of government trading policy—e.g. joining a common market—may influence the marginal propensity to consume domestically produced goods *vis-à-vis* the marginal propensity to import. For the present, however, we will content ourselves with the observation that even an elementary model of national income determination as we have used here is capable of providing insights into possible policy action.

III. EXTENSION TO THE GOVERNMENT SECTOR

As a first step toward making the model more realistic we will now allow for the role of government. We will, however, still retain the assumption of a closed economy for the moment. Also we will make the simplifying assumptions that government expenditures are autonomous and income tax rates proportional to income. Despite the elementary nature of the model it will be found that the policy implications are considerable.

The basic national income identity is now represented by $Y \equiv C + I + G$, where the final symbol stands for government spending. Consumption will now be a linear function of income after the payment of taxes and the receipt of transfers. Thus $C = \alpha + bY^d$ where Y^d indicates disposable income. Disposable income is given by the equation $Y^d = -\eta + (1 - t_y)Y + R$ where t_y equals the rate of income tax, R represents transfer payments, for simplicity assumed non-taxable, and η represents that portion of taxation which continues even though income is zero—e.g. taxes upon property. Our national income model is thus represented by the following system of equations:

$$Y = C + I + G$$
$$C = \alpha + bY^d$$
$$Y^d = -\eta + (1 - t_y)Y + R$$
$$I = \bar{I}$$
$$G = \bar{G}$$

which yields the equation for the equilibrium level of national income as

$$Y = \frac{\alpha - \eta b + bR + \bar{I} + \bar{G}}{1 - b + bt_y} \qquad (\text{II.2})$$

As before, we will examine some of the multipliers that can be obtained from the model. Initially we will assume that the rate of income taxation is zero, i.e. that all government revenue stems from, let us say, property taxation, η. In this case our national income equation reduces to

$$Y = \frac{\alpha - \eta b + bR + \bar{I} + \bar{G}}{1 - b} \qquad (\text{II.2a})$$

Now the government expenditures multiplier, for an autonomous change in government spending upon goods and services, is given by $dY/dG = 1/(1-b)$. Again it will be noted that this is identical to the result obtained from an autonomous change in investment or in the constant term in the consumption function of the same amount; thus $dY/dG = dY/dI = dY/d\alpha$. For our present purposes, however, we wish to concentrate upon the government sector. Let us now examine the effect of an autonomous change in property taxation upon the level of national income. In this case $dY/d\eta = -b/(1-b)$ which provides us with the tax multiplier. The expression is of course negative; an increase in the rate of property taxation will depress the income level and vice versa. If we now ask what is the combined effect of an equal change in both government spending and taxation, we at once have

The Static Theory of Fiscal Policy: Closed Economy

$$dY = \frac{\delta Y}{\delta G} \cdot dG + \frac{\delta Y}{\delta \eta} \cdot d\eta$$

$$= \left(\frac{1}{1-b}\right) dG + \left(\frac{-b}{1-b}\right) d\eta$$

$$= \left(\frac{1-b}{1-b}\right) dG = dG$$

This is the well-known Haavelmo-Gelting balanced budget theorem which demonstrates that an equal change in expenditures and taxes—so that the condition of the budget surplus or deficit remains unchanged—will not be neutral upon the level of national income. In the above case, the increase in the level of national income is precisely equal to the change in government spending—the multiplier is unity. This example is dependent upon the observation of the somewhat stringent assumptions of the model and must for all practical policy purposes be substantially modified. Nonetheless, before proceeding to consider some of the more important modifications it is well to dwell upon the significance of this result. In the first place it provides the theoretical vindication of the annually balanced budget. Paradoxically, it is in fact the *Keynesian* justification of non-deficit finance, for, given the assumptions and limitations of the analysis, it demonstrates that it is always possible to secure the full employment level of income without incurring a budget deficit provided one is prepared to increase the size of the budget sufficiently. It is ironic that the proponents of annually balanced budgets are invariably the advocates of limiting the size of the government sector, for clearly the two diverse positions are not necessarily consistent with the maintenance of full employment income. Secondly, the argument illustrates that an increase in government spending will normally exert a more high-powered impact upon the level of national income than a comparable decrease in taxes. A government concerned with the trade-off between full employment income and budget deficit should logically favour the former alternative. However, since consumers are prone to identify more strongly with the benefits of decreased taxation than with those of government expenditure, a government concerned with the trade-off between deficit finance and electoral appeal may well adopt the latter alternative.

Having indicated the importance of the basic theory, let us now consider some of the more important qualifications. To begin with we must dispense with the assumption that income tax rates are zero. In this case the government expenditures multiplier becomes $dY/dG = 1/(1 - b + bt_y)$ and the tax multiplier is now $dY/d\eta = -b/(1 - b + bt_y)$ so that the combined effect of an equal change in both expenditures and property taxation is now

$$\left(\frac{1}{1 - b + bt_y}\right)dG + \left(\frac{-b}{1 - b + bt_y}\right)d\eta = \left(\frac{1 - b}{1 - b + bt_y}\right)dG$$

Accordingly, in this instance where taxes are dependent upon the level of income the balanced budget multiplier is less than unity; the higher the rate of tax the lower the value of the multiplier.[4] However, one may logically raise the objection that we are no longer dealing with a balanced budget multiplier since, clearly if taxes are dependent upon income, an increase in national income will raise taxes over and above the initial indirect tax levy. The budget, if previously balanced, would now show a fiscal surplus. This raises the issues of how a balanced budget change should be defined, and in particular if induced changes in tax yields are to be taken into account. What then is the relevant time period for purposes of analysis?

A second important modification revolves around the nature of the government spending. Thus far we have assumed that the spending has been directly incurred upon the purchase of goods and services. If, however, we were to assume that the government utilized the tax revenues to provide transfer payments to members of the population at large we would no longer be employing the government expenditures multiplier. Instead we would be using the government transfers multiplier which is $dY/dR = b/(1 - b + bt_y)$.

In this case, the impact of an increase in taxes matched by an equal increase in government transfer payments yields

$$\left(\frac{-b}{1 - b + bt_y}\right)d\eta + \left(\frac{b}{1 - b + bt_y}\right)dR = 0$$

There would be no change upon the equilibrium level of national income as long as the marginal propensity to consume of the taxpayers was equal to the marginal propensity to consume of the transfer recipients. This conclusion is of course one which accords with common sense. If the government were to levy taxes on the one hand and immediately repay the proceeds to the taxpayer on the other, then ignoring administrative costs, time lags and so forth, we would expect no repercussion upon the level of national income. For this reason, transfer payments are commonly looked upon as negative taxes in conventional analysis. In practice, government expenditures encompass both purchases of goods and services and also transfer payments. Accordingly, we have two reasons for believing that the balanced budget multiplier will in fact be less than unity: firstly, because, as we have shown, tax receipts are normally dependent upon income levels and, secondly, because a portion of the government expenditure will exert no income-generating impact.

To invoke other qualifications to the principle of the balanced budget multiplier at this stage is to go beyond the confines of the present model, but for the sake of continuity it is perhaps as well to indicate them briefly. If we dispense with the assumption that investment expenditures are autonomous then the multiplier may be reinforced by induced income changes—and also possibly by the complementary nature of government purchases. Alternatively, a competitive relationship between government purchases and private investment would reduce the size of the multiplier. Thus, before one can estimate the magnitude of the balanced budget multiplier one would need to know the nature of the government spending programme. The erection of pyramids upon Salisbury Plain would no doubt exert a greater income-generating impact than an equivalent expenditure which might otherwise be undertaken by the private sector.

As previously observed, the simple balanced budget multiplier formula, with zero income taxes and autonomous investment expenditure, generates an income change precisely equal to the change in government expenditure. The multiplier is unity and this holds regardless of the value of the marginal propensity to consume prevailing in the private sector—provided it is less than one. One consequence is that the extension of the model to an open economy in no way affects the basic outcome as long as government expenditures fall entirely upon domestic output. This situation, whereby the private sector is responsible for total imports, is then merely akin to an autonomous decline in the marginal propensity to consume leaving the balanced budget multiplier unchanged. If, however, the government sector also imports, then this conclusion is immediately modified. The greater the percentage of tax revenues utilized for imports, the smaller will be the income generating impact. Indeed, if the marginal importing propensity of the public sector exceeds that of the private, then it is theoretically possible for the balanced budget multiplier to be negative. This situation may have relevance to less advanced economies where the importing propensity of the private sector may be low—with prohibitive tariffs and quotas upon consumer goods—whilst that of the public sector may be comparatively high especially when the latter is a large importer of capital goods.

Finally, another qualification to the balanced budget multiplier arises from a consideration of government expenditures upon goods and services which are then given *free of charge* to needy recipients. If the latter experience an income gain, which will normally be the case, they may attempt to modify their savings patterns and, since it is virtually impossible to save out of payments in kind, this will generally entail saving out of alternative income. In the extreme, if unlikely, case whereby they value the service provision as equal to its cost, and if they possess identical marginal consumption propensities to those of the taxpayer, there will be no impact upon the equilibrium level of national income.[5] When all these factors are taken into account, it is clear that a balanced budget multiplier with a value equal to unity is but a special case, though a not unimportant one.

Despite the comparative simplicity of the present model, the allowance of a government sector financed by a proportional income tax permits us to demonstrate a number of issues decidedly pertinent to fiscal policy. First of all, let us consider the principle of automatic stabilization. With a proportional income tax the multiplier for, say, an autonomous change in investment expenditures is given by $1/(1 - b + bt_y)$. Without income taxation, the multiplier as we have seen is simply $1/(1 - b)$. A proportional income tax, therefore, is an automatic stabilizer to the extent that it reduces the size of the multiplier. The extent to which it is a stabilizing device may be estimated simply by comparing the size of the two multipliers. Thus

$$\frac{1}{(1-b)} - \frac{1}{(1-b+bt_y)} = \frac{bt_y}{(1-b)^2 + bt_y(1-b)}$$

which provides us with a measure of the proportional income tax as a stabilizing device. Clearly, the element of automatic stabilization is greater, the greater the rate of taxation; increasing the tax rate reduces the multiplier until, in the extreme case where the tax rate is 100 per cent, the multiplier is reduced to unity. Before concluding that the tax structure with the higher tax rate is preferable from the stabilization viewpoint it must be remembered that automatic stabilizers cut both ways. Decreasing the size of the multiplier reduces the effectiveness of counter-cyclical government spending. The concept of an automatic stabilizer, therefore, is really something of a mixed blessing; it decreases the extent of cyclical fluctuations but it also retards the movement towards recovery.

As we have just seen, an increase in the rate of tax reduces the size of the multiplier and thereby raises the element of automatic stabilization. Since the multiplier, in this case, is given by $k = 1/(1 - b + bt_y)$ the effect of a tax change may be summarized simply as

$$\frac{dk}{dt_y} = \frac{-b}{(1 - b + bt_y)^2}$$

which in turn we may express as $-bk^2$. The relationship, as we would expect, is negative. An increase in the rate of income tax will, other things remaining equal, decrease the size of the multiplier. The decrease itself will be greater, the larger the marginal propensity to consume and also will be greater, the larger the size of the multiplier—providing the latter is greater than one. Since we are assuming that the values of both b and t_y fall between 0 and 1, this will always be the case. Thus, in the present case, the mathematical results would accord with our intuitive guesses.

A far less obvious conclusion to be derived from the model, however, is the impact of the change in the rate of tax upon the extent of any fiscal deficit associated with an increased government expenditure.[6] An increase in government expenditure implies, *ceteris paribus,* an increase in the size of the budget deficit (or a decrease in the size of the fiscal surplus). The extent of the deficit will normally be less than the increased government expenditure, however, since the induced expansion of income will automatically generate higher tax revenues. It is for this reason that the financial costs of an investment undertaken by the government sector may justifiably be judged less than those that would be incurred if the project were carried out by the private sector; to a certain extent government public works will be self-financing.[7] Thus we may write

$$\Delta D = \Delta G - \Delta T$$

where D represents the budget deficit and T government tax receipts. Given a proportional income tax, t_y, ΔT is equal to

$\Delta Y t_y$ and in turn ΔY will be given by ΔGk where k is the multiplier and equal in the present case to $1/(1-b+bt_y)$. Thus

$$\begin{aligned}\Delta D &= \Delta G - \Delta Gkt_y \\ &= \Delta G(1-kt_y)\end{aligned} \qquad (\text{II.3})$$

What we wish to know is how will the increase in the deficit respond to a change in the rate of income taxation? The answer is by no means obvious. On the one hand, as we have already seen, an increased tax rate will limit the extent of income expansion by reducing the size of the multiplier. On the other hand, a higher tax rate will automatically raise the level of receipts from any given level of income. Which effect will predominate? What we require is the sign of $d\Delta D/dt_y$ which is given by

$$\frac{d}{dt_y} \Delta G(1-kt_y)$$

But for the purpose of the argument we may dispense with ΔG by simply assuming it to be unity; such a procedure in no way modifies the qualitative conclusion. Thus we take

$$\frac{d}{dt_y}(1-kt_y) = -\left(\frac{dk}{dt_y} \cdot t_y + \frac{dt_y}{dt_y} \cdot k\right)$$

Since we already know the value of dk/dt_y to be $-bk^2$ this reduces to

$$\begin{aligned}\frac{d}{dt_y}(1-kt_y) &= bt_y k^2 - k \\ &= k(bt_y k - 1)\end{aligned} \qquad (\text{II.3a})$$

This expression is negative since we have previously assumed b to fall between the values of 0 and 1 and kt_y must be less than 1 since we have previously defined the increase in the deficit as $\Delta G - \Delta Gkt_y$. Thus we conclude that for any given increase in government expenditure, tax rates and increased deficits are inversely related; a raising of the tax rate reduces the extent of the higher deficit, and vice versa. This in turn implies that the enhanced revenue yield from any given income level more than offsets the decline in the value of the multiplier.

A closely related question to the above involves the effect of a change in the tax rate upon the total revenue yield. Again, there are two opposing effects to consider; the higher tax rate increases the yield from any given income level whilst at the same time reducing the level of income by lowering the value of the multiplier. Since, as we have just demonstrated in the deficit case, the higher tax rate more than offsets the decline in the multiplier, we would expect an increase in the rate of tax to increase total revenue yields. This is in fact the case as we can show simply in the following way:

$$T = t_y Y$$

$$Y = kZ$$

where we allow Z to stand for the sum of all autonomous expenditures. Therefore

$$T = t_y k Z$$

and

$$\frac{dT}{dt_y} = \left[\frac{dt_y}{dt_y} \cdot k + \frac{dk}{dt_y} \cdot t_y\right] Z$$

$$= [k - bt_y k^2] Z$$

$$= [k(1 - bt_y k)] Z \tag{II.4}$$

Since we have previously found the expression $k(bt_y k - 1)$ to be negative, expression II.4 will be positive for any positive value of Z. Thus, raising the tax rate will increase the revenue yield. The reader need hardly be reminded that the above analysis abstracts from any induced incentive effects. Nonetheless, this result provides an interesting contrast to the case of a sales tax. With the latter, the assumption of normally shaped demand curves leads to the conclusion that there is some effective rate of tax which serves to maximize the total revenue yield. Beyond this point, higher tax rates so depress consumption that total tax revenue falls and would ultimately decline to zero. Diagrammatically, we may express this as in Figure II.1 where tax rate t_0 maximizes tax yield. It follows that if the authorities imposing the tax have some concept of a target yield to be obtained from taxing this particular commodity they will have a choice of tax rate for any target income other than the maximum one. Thus if the target yield is OT, then either tax rate t_1 or t_2 would accomplish the objective. Which rate is chosen will depend upon whether or not consumption of the good is to be encouraged. This result stems directly from the fact that the tax yield does possess a maximum value. In contrast, in the case of an income tax—at least within the confines of the present model—no such maximum value can exist. No area of discretion exists with regard to the tax rate required to meet any given target income.

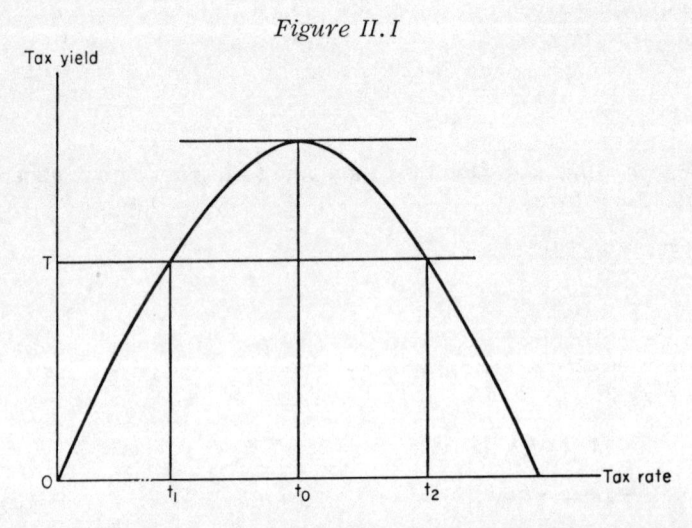

Figure II.I

[Figure II.I: A parabolic curve showing Tax yield on the vertical axis versus Tax rate on the horizontal axis. The curve rises from origin O, reaches a maximum at t_0, and returns to the axis. A horizontal line at height T intersects the curve at t_1 and t_2.]

The foregoing has indicated some of the consequences of extending the simple Keynesian model to the government sector. Other implications could be derived. However, beyond a point, successive applications of similar techniques are subject to rapidly diminishing returns, for our objective is not to squeeze every last pip from each successive offering, but rather, by the gradual relinquishing of assumptions and by the extension of the analysis of other sectors, to develop a more realistic aid for the application of fiscal policy.

IV. EXTENSION TO THE MONETARY SECTOR

It is not without significance that Keynes included the word 'money' in his title of the *General Theory*, for he wanted to show that money was important in the determination of national income. This was in sharp contrast to the classical tradition. In the classical world, money was merely a veil which one had to first penetrate before confronting the 'real forces' at work within the

The Static Theory of Fiscal Policy: Closed Economy

economy. Money had a role to play—and indeed a most significant role—in the determination of the absolute price level but it exercised no importance whatsoever in the determination of relative prices or of national output and employment. For Keynes, on the other hand, the volume of money was a major force in the determination of the rate of interest, which in turn had a crucial role in determining the volume of investment and hence of national income. In view of this, it is strange that so many expositions of the Keynesian theory of fiscal policy ignore the monetary sector. Our earlier exposition was in keeping with this recent convention. What we wish to do now is to extend our analysis to allow for the monetary factor and to indicate its importance for our generalized national-income model. In so doing, we will be taking an essential first step towards enlarging our model to include the external capital sector, for it cannot be denied that domestic interest rates exercise a profound effect upon the overall balance of payments position.

In order to introduce the monetary sector, we must first distinguish between the goods market and the money market. With regard to the former, our system of equations is virtually the same as before but now we must allow for investment spending being dependent, to some extent, upon the rate of interest. For simplicity we will assume that investment is a linear function of the rate of interest so that $I = \beta - qi$ where β is the investment demand at zero interest and i represents the rate of interest. The relation is, of course, negative. It is assumed that an increase in the rate of interest will curtail the volume of investment. Accordingly our system of equations will now be:

$$Y = C + I + G$$
$$C = \alpha + bY^d$$
$$Y^d = -\eta + (1 - t_y)Y + R$$
$$I = \beta - qi$$
$$G = \bar{G}$$

and the equilibrium level of national income will be given by the equation

$$Y = \frac{\alpha - \eta b + bR + \beta - qi + \bar{G}}{1 - b + bt_y} \tag{II.5}$$

Now, in addition to all the other variables specified before, we need to know the rate of interest in order to determine the equilibrium level of income. We can no longer determine this question without appealing to the money market. The equation specified above corresponds to the Hicks-Hansen IS function.

In order to consider the money market we shall adopt the Keynesian position that the demand for money may be broadly divided into two general categories: the transactions and precautionary demand upon the one hand and the speculative demand upon the other. The former we shall regard as being proportional to national income; the latter we shall assume to be an inverse function of the rate of interest. Thus we have

$$L = L^t + L^s$$
$$L^t = vY$$
$$L^s = \gamma - ci$$
$$L = vY + \gamma - ci$$

where L^t and L^s are the transactions and speculative demand respectively, being equal to the total monetary demand L, and where γ is the amount of speculative balances held when interest rates are zero.

Equilibrium requires that the money stock, fixed exogenously by the banking sector, equals the total monetary demand so that

$$MS = vY + \gamma - ci$$

where MS represents the fixed stock of money. We can now express the above equation in terms of the rate of interest as

$$i = \frac{vY + \gamma - MS}{c}$$

which we may regard as equivalent to the Hicks-Hansen LM function.

We now have two sets of simultaneous equations which may be solved for equilibrium. From the goods market we have

$$Y = \frac{\alpha - \eta b + bR + \beta - qi + \bar{G}}{1 - b + bt_y}$$

and from the money market we have

$$i = \frac{vY + \gamma - MS}{c}$$

from which we may derive our solution for the equilibrium level of income as

$$Y = \frac{\alpha - \eta b + bR + \beta - q\left[(\gamma/c) - (MS/c)\right] + \bar{G}}{1 - b + bt_y + (qv/c)} \quad \text{(II. 6)}$$

The above equation, which corresponds to the Hicks-Hansen solution for the equilibrium level of national income, may appear somewhat complex. For our present purposes, however, it is sufficient to consider the relevant multipliers. The government expenditures multiplier is now given by

$$\frac{dY}{dG} = \frac{1}{1 - b + bt_y + (qv/c)} \quad \text{(II. 6a)}$$

Thus by allowing for the money market we have modified our original expenditures multiplier to the extent of the final term in the denominator qv/c. This means that an increase in government spending will normally exert less influence than before, since the expansion of national income will be accompanied by increased demands for transactions cash raising the rate of interest. As long as the investment demand function is at all interest-elastic some offsetting decrease in private investment will occur.[8] The same general conclusion applies to all our multipliers. For any given change in expenditures, whether by the government or the private sector, the multiplier will be less than before. Thus the monetary sector incorporates its own degree of built-in stability. With a fixed money stock, any expansion of income will be accompanied by a raising of interest rates; any decrease of income should be accompanied by a corresponding fall at least until the floor level of interest rates is reached. This element of automatic monetary stability will be reinforced if price movements accompany the income change, for the transactions demand should more properly be regarded as a function of the monetary level of income. Given the institutional fact that prices tend to reveal downward inflexibility, it is reasonable to conclude that automatic monetary stability will be more potent in expansionary periods than in recession. However, the comparative strength of this factor in expansionary or contractionary periods is not our main concern. It is sufficient to note that it serves as an automatic offset to fiscal policy generally. For fiscal policy to be fully effective, therefore, it should be accompanied by monetary policy designed to neutralize the induced changes in liquidity conditions. In particular, what we wish to stress here is that to examine fiscal policy in a vacuum without regard to monetary conditions or repercussions is a procedure which may well invite serious error.

The preceding multiplier (II.6.1) typifies the Keynesian approach to fiscal policy. Implicitly, it assumes that the government expenditure is financed by an expansion of national debt—i.e. by the sale of government bonds to the public in exchange for cash. When the government spends the proceeds the money supply is returned to its former level and, of course, there is no change in taxation—hence the rationale for summing up the total impact solely in terms of $\frac{dY}{dG}$. However, this approach assumes that there is no repercussion arising from the increased bondholding by the private sector. In fact, the private sector is likely to look upon both its holding of money and its holding of government bonds as assets entering into private sector wealth. With no change in the volume of money in circulation but with an increase in the holding of government bonds, the fiscal change summarized in (II.6.1) will imply a net increase in private sector wealth. Thus increase in private wealth will generate additional effects. On the one hand, it will generate an increase in consumer spending if the latter responds to changes in net worth as implied in the celebrated Pigou effect. This will reinforce the outward shift of the IS function initiated by the increased government expenditure. But if consumption responds to changes in net worth then logically so too will the demand for money—assuming money is not an inferior good. Accordingly, there will arise an induced inward shift of the LM function offsetting in part the fiscal impact. It is partly for these reasons that monetarists have remained sceptical about the impact of fiscal intervention and have criticized the 'Keynesian' school for concentrating only upon the initial impact and for ignoring the induced reaction upon the LM curve.[9] To take account of the wealth effect described above would imply restating the income change in terms of the total differential, thus:

$$dY = \frac{\partial Y}{\partial G} \cdot dG + \frac{\partial Y}{\partial W} \cdot dW$$

Whether the fiscal impact is offset or not depends upon whether consumption spending or the demand for money is more responsive to changes in private sector wealth; in either case the position is complicated by the need to allow for changes in the price of government bonds as interest rates rise—implying negative wealth effects for existing bondholders.

If we specifically assume no change in the *volume* of outstanding government debt then the increased government expenditure will have to be financed in one of two ways: by an equal increase in taxation or alternatively by an increase in the money supply.

The ultimate multiplier will incorporate not only the government expenditures multiplier, but also the subsequent changes consequent upon the method of finance. In the first case, that of a balanced budget change, the total impact is given by

$$dY = \frac{\partial Y}{\partial G} \cdot dG + \frac{\partial Y}{\partial \eta} \cdot d\eta = \frac{1-b}{1-b+bt_y+(qv/c)} \; . \quad (\text{II.7})$$

assuming the tax change occurs in the autonomous component. In the second case, that of monetary expansion, the final impact will be

$$dY = \frac{\partial Y}{\partial G} \cdot dG + \frac{\partial Y}{\gamma MS} \cdot dMS = \frac{1+(q/c)}{1-b+bt_y+(qv/c)} \quad (\text{II.8})$$

which, as we would expect, is greater than the above.

In comparing these methods of finance, it is clear that the monetary expansion method will be the most powerful, for in this case the expansionary effects of increased expenditure will be reinforced by induced investment from the private sector as interest rates fall. The method of debt finance will normally be the second most potent means of financing increased expenditure, although a more realistic analysis would have to allow for changes in the age profile of the outstanding debt and possible repercussions upon the lending ability of the banking sector. Within the framework of our present model, however, the only offset to the expansionary influence of increased government expenditure arises from the induced rise in interest rates as the transactions demand for money increases along with national income. Clearly, the balanced budget method is the most restrictive, for with no change in the debt or the money stock the entire burden of finance falls upon increased tax revenues with a consequent decline in consumer expenditure.

These issues are closely related to the modern-day monetarist argument that the impact of fiscal action upon macrovariables depends crucially upon the method of finance. The contention is that expenditure financed by taxation has little net impact; all that is involved is a transfer of purchasing power from the private to the public sector. With regard to the issue of new securities, interest rates are raised with unfavourable implications for private investment spending and also negative wealth effects suffered by existing bondholders with possibly adverse impacts upon consumption. In contrast, expenditure financed by the creation of new money is devoid of these constraints, its greater impact upon the aggregate economy providing the rationale for the assertion (hotly denied) that it is monetary action, not fiscal change, which is vital for stabilization policy. Our purpose is not to enter into the money versus fiscal control debate, apart from perhaps commenting that much of the heat of that particular controversy appears to be generated by the difficulties of adequately defining fiscal and monetary action independently of each other.

Thus, consideration of the monetary sector not only modifies our original findings by emphasizing the element of automatic monetary stability, but also highlights the importance of alternative means of finance. We will also find that the monetary sector has a vital role to play in adjustments to the international balance of payments. We will delay consideration of this issue, however, until we have examined the operation of the simple static model in an open economy which is the subject matter of the following chapter.

NOTES

(1) It will be noted here, and indeed throughout the volume, that we have followed the familiar short cut of obtaining the equilibrium level of national income by substituting *ex ante* relationships into an *ex post* identity. Strictly speaking, such a procedure is only permissible if we add the necessary equilibrium condition of the equality between *ex ante* and *ex post* values: in the present case, for example, that 'desired' equals actual consumption. We assume that readers of this volume will be sufficiently familiar with this distinction to permit us to avoid repetition of the required equilibrium conditions. For a particularly clear discussion of this distinction see Gardner Ackley, *Macroeconomic Theory*, Macmillan, New York, 1961.

(2) In terms of economic growth, however, it might make a considerable difference whether the change was in investment or consumption spending.

The Static Theory of Fiscal Policy: Closed Economy 43

(3) A possible exception to this statement was the British adoption of premium bonds which presumably was an attempt to increase saving by changing both average and marginal propensities.

(4) Less obviously, the multiplier will be greater the lower the value of the marginal propensity to consume and vice versa!

(5) Cf. A. T. Peacock. 'The Multiplier and the Valuation of Government Expenditures', *Finanz Archiv*, Band 30, Heft 3, 1972, which deals with a range of cases of this kind.

(6) The discussion here follows closely G. C. Archibald and Richard G. Lipsey, *An Introduction to a Mathematical Treatment of Economics*, 2nd edn, Weidenfeld and Nicolson, London, 1973.

(7) The opportunity cost in terms of the use of scarce resources will, of course, be identical.

(8) If the investment demand function is completely inelastic, q becomes zero. In this case, investment is again autonomously determined so that $\beta = I$ and the multiplier is as before. It follows that the money market is of no significance to the equilibrium level of national income. However, we have reached the classical conclusion by invoking an investment demand function that the classical economist would hardly have considered.

(9) See A. S. Blinder and R. M. Solow, 'Does Fiscal Policy Matter?', *Journal of Public Economics*, Nov. 1973.

Chapter III

THE STATIC THEORY OF FISCAL POLICY: OPEN ECONOMY

I. INTRODUCTION

In this chapter we shall take an important step towards a more realistic framework for fiscal policy proposals by extending the analysis to the external sector. We shall find that income determination, and hence fiscal policy variables, are now interdependent as between countries. Moreover, by extending the analysis to the international trading sector we are able to consider what is perhaps the most powerful constraint upon domestic policy measures—namely the international balance of payments. We shall treat this topic in two stages: firstly we shall consider the balance of trade, i.e. the relation between exports and imports, leaving the monetary sector aside; secondly, we shall complete the analysis by specifically allowing for the influence of interest rates upon international capital movements. Before concluding the static framework we will add a comment upon the multiplier analysis and discuss briefly some limitations and shortcomings of the analysis.

II. THE TWO-COUNTRY MODEL

When dealing with the external sector the first difficulty we encounter is that we can no longer consider one country in isolation. Hitherto, we have used only one national income identity; now we must be prepared to consider a series of multiple equations for each and every country entering into international trade. The complexity of the model that would be required to approximate the conditions of the real world would be enormous; simplification is essential.

Fortunately, we can render the analysis far more tractable by assuming that there are only two countries entering into world trade. For expositional purposes this is a perfectly permissible assumption, since conceptually we can always divide the world into two trading blocs: the country under consideration and 'the rest of the world'. Moreover, such a procedure has one compelling and

The Static Theory of Fiscal Policy: Open Economy

overriding virtue in that, when we are dealing with a two-country model, it is definitionally true that the imports of one are automatically equal to the exports of the other. As we shall see, this identity is of paramount importance to the analysis which follows. In addition, we can simplify the algebraic manipulation still further by dispensing with the existence of lump sum taxes (property taxation in our previous illustrations) and with government transfer payments. These aids were invoked solely to expound the balanced budget multiplier theorem; to dispense with them prevents our system of equations from becoming too encumbered symbolically whilst in no way modifying the general nature of our conclusions.

We denote our two countries by the letters A and B. We now have two national income identities as follows, where the symbols X and M denote exports and imports respectively and where the subscripts refer to the country concerned:

$$Y_a \equiv C_a + I_a + G_a + X_a - M_a$$

$$Y_b \equiv C_b + I_b + G_b + X_b - M_b$$

We assume that imports into country A are a function of disposable income within country A. Thus $M_a = j_a Y_a^d$ where j_a is the marginal propensity to import of country A. For simplicity, we ignore imports at zero income. Since within our two country framework, the imports of country A are equal to the exports of country B, it follows that

$$X_b = j_a Y_a^d$$

Likewise, we may write

$$M_b = X_a = j_b Y_b^d$$

For the moment we will ignore the monetary sector. Thus our national income model for country A will be represented by the following set of equations:

$$Y_a = C_a + I_a + G_a + X_a - M_a$$

$$C_a = \alpha_a + b_a Y_a^d$$

$$Y_a^d = Y_a(1 - t_{ya})$$

$$I_a = \bar{I}_a$$

$$G_a = \bar{G}_a$$

$$X_a = j_b Y_b(1 - t_{yb})$$

$$M_a = j_a Y_a(1 - t_{ya})$$

$$Z_a = \alpha_a + \bar{I}_a + \bar{G}_a$$

Solving for Y_a provides us with the equilibrium level of national income for country A:

$$Y_a = \frac{Z_a + j_b Y_b(1 - t_{yb})}{1 - b_a + b_a t_{ya} + j_a - j_a t_{ya}} \qquad \text{(III.1)}$$

To simplify slightly, let us write

$$k_a = \frac{1}{1 - b_a + b_a t_{ya} + j_a - j_a t_{ya}}$$

where k_a may be considered a 'domestic' multiplier determining the impact of any autonomous expenditure in country A in the absence of any induced foreign repercussion from country B. Thus we now have

$$Y_a = k_a[Z_a + j_b Y_b(1 - t_{yb})] \qquad \text{(III.1a)}$$

It follows that we can no longer determine the national income of country A without prior knowledge of conditions pertaining in country B.[1] The income level, tax rates and marginal importing propensities of country B are all factors which enter into the national income determination of country A.

Reversal of the subscripts provides us with an identical income equation for country B and solving the two simultaneous equations yields a determinate solution for the model:

$$Y_a = \frac{k_a[Z_a + j_b k_b Z_b(1 - t_{yb})]}{1 - k_b k_a j_b j_a(1 - t_{ya} - t_{yb} + t_{ya}t_{yb})} \qquad \text{(III.2a)}$$

$$Y_b = \frac{k_b[Z_b + j_a k_a Z_a(1 - t_{ya})]}{1 - k_a k_b j_a j_b(1 - t_{yb} - t_{ya} + t_{yb}t_{ya})} \qquad \text{(III.2b)}$$

In what follows we will deal only in terms of country A but it will be appreciated that the argument is equally applicable to country B. With regard to country A, income changes are now not simply a function of changes arising internally but are also dependent upon autonomous and policy variables in country B. We may express this mathematically in terms of the total differential, thus:

$$dY_a = \frac{\partial Y_a}{\partial \theta} \cdot d\theta + \frac{\partial Y_a}{\partial \phi} \cdot d\phi \qquad \text{(III. 3)}$$

where θ and ϕ are shift parameters encompassing all possible changes arising in the respective countries. If the level of income in country A is such that A's objective macro-function is being maximized, subject to whatever constraints exist, then the job of fiscal policy is to neutralize parameter shifts in B so that the total differential is maintained at zero. To the extent that such disturbances emanating from B are not offset by fiscal policy in A they serve as a destabilizing influence.

To bring out some of the implications in more detail, let us examine the multiplier for an autonomous change in spending in country A. In this case we have

$$\frac{\partial Y_a}{\partial Z_a} = \frac{k_a}{1 - k_b k_a j_b j_a (1 - t_{ya} - t_{yb} + t_{ya} t_{yb})} \qquad \text{(III. 4)}$$

Now if we momentarily assume the value of j_b to be zero, the multiplier is immediately reduced to k_a which is clearly less than the above for all $0 < j_b, j_a, t_{ya}, t_{yb} < 1$.[2] Thus the marginal propensity to import of country B is but one factor which magnifies the income-generating impact of autonomous expenditure in country A. This is because the process of income expansion in country A induces income growth in B by stimulating the export sector of the latter. In turn higher income levels in B exert a feedback effect upon the export industries of country A. It follows that an autonomous increase in the marginal importing propensity in B will, of its own accord, exert income-generating changes in country A. This issue is of some importance to the formation of common markets, since it is likely that importing propensities will increase for the member nations. The implication that destabilizing income movements are more likely to be transmitted between the partners to an economic union may be influential in stimulating concerted stabilization policies.[3]

Other examples and implications for fiscal interdependence could be derived from the basic model. However, it is sufficient to note that extension of the analysis to the external sector modifies our earlier multiplier concepts by diminishing the size of domestic multipliers in favour of increased external impacts upon other nations. From the viewpoint of any one country experiencing autonomous income changes, the open economy appears as a stabilizer; for the rest of the world it is destabilizing. In either case, just as it is necessary to consider monetary conditions in the formulation of fiscal policies it is equally necessary to take account of the external sector.

III. THE BALANCE OF TRADE

One fundamental reason for dealing with the external sector is the fact that it brings into full conflict the choice between the maintenance of full employment income and balance of payments equilibria. We wish to highlight the conflict here by demonstrating that a country initiating an expansion of income will find the resulting increase in imports exceeding the induced increase in exports.[4]

We wish to show that $(dX_a - dM_a)/dY_a$ is negative. To facilitate the exposition we shall assume that income tax rates are zero. In this case we know that

$$\frac{dM_a}{dY_a} = j_a > 0$$

and exports of country A, in equilibrium, are given by

$$X_a = j_b Y_b$$

Thus we may write

$$X_a = j_b k_b (Z_b + j_a Y_a)$$

and

$$\frac{dX_a}{dY_a} = \frac{j_b j_a}{1 - b_b + j_b}$$

since k_b now equals $1/(1 - b_b + j_b)$. Both dM_a/dY_a and dX_a/dY_a are positive, the former owing to the assumption of a positive marginal importing propensity and the latter due to the element of foreign repercussion. Our concern is with the sign of

$$\frac{j_b j_a}{(1 - b_b + j_b)} - j_a$$

This we may write as

$$j_a \left(\frac{j_b}{1 - b_b + j_b} - 1 \right)$$

Now as long as $j_b/(1 - b_b + j_b) < 1$ the total expression must be negative but this will always be the case if the marginal propensity to consume in country B is less than unity for then the denominator must always exceed the numerator. Accordingly, we may conclude that domestic expansion will, *ceteris paribus,* always lead to a worsening of the balance of trade by generating imports in excess of the induced expansion of exports. This is a qualitative conclusion of profound importance to the theory of fiscal policy.

Paradoxically, this is a finding which has been responsible for a certain neglect of the external sector in models of national income determination. For our conclusion, that domestic income expansion leads to a deterioration of the balance of trade, would have been obtained equally well had we initially assumed exports to be exogenously determined. Such an assumption is frequently adopted when extending the Keynesian income formulation to the foreign trading sector; it permits valid qualitative conclusions to be reached and it avoids the need to consider foreign income levels and the problem of simultaneous income adjustments. For certain purposes such a procedure is entirely permissible and it is one that we ourselves shall adopt in subsequent treatments. It should always be remembered, however, that fiscal policy effects do not heed national frontiers and the element of repercussion can never be entirely absent. Moreover, there is a danger that single-country models may identify the balance of trade too strongly with the balance of payments and thus abstract entirely from international capital movements. It is to this topic that we now turn.

IV. THE BALANCE OF PAYMENTS

In this section we make a return to the method of analysis of Chapter II where we showed the need to integrate both the commodity and money markets to determine full equilibrium. The Hicks—Hansen solution demonstrated the importance of the money market in providing for an element of automatic stability. With a fixed money stock, it was shown that an expansion of income would automatically lead to a raising of the interest rate through the renewed demand for transactions balances. In Chapter II we were concerned with the impact of higher interest rates upon the level of domestic activity. Now, however, we wish to extend the Hicks-Hansen analysis to allow for the external sector.

We have previously shown that an expansion of national income will generate increased imports in excess of induced exports. This is the balance-of-trade effect of income expansion. When considering the balance of payments, however, we must also allow for the capital account. The Hicks-Hansen analysis would suggest that income expansion would aid the capital account by raising interest rates since it is assumed that $dB^K/di > 0$ where B^K stands for the capital account of the balance of payments. If this is the case, it follows that we can make no definite prediction of the impact of income expansion upon the overall balance of payments. Letting B stand for the overall balance of payments we may express this as

$$B = X - M + B^K$$

$$\frac{dM}{dY} > 0$$

$$\frac{dX - dM}{dY} < 0$$

$$\frac{dB^K}{di} > 0$$

$$\frac{dB^K}{dY} > 0$$

$$\therefore \frac{dB}{dY} \lesseqgtr 0$$

Admittedly, the above analysis is decidedly partial. When considering capital movements we are more properly concerned with the differential change in interest rates between countries. Income expansion in country A will, by generating similar movements in the income level of country B, lead to a raising of interest rates in the latter country. Normally one would expect this effect to be far weaker in the country experiencing the induced impact but in the last resort the net impact will be determined by the comparative demand functions for money in the respective economies. Granted the qualification, it is still true that, just as we must consider monetary conditions in the formulation of domestic fiscal policies, so too must we take account of international capital movements when we extend the analysis to the international sector.

We can perhaps highlight the implications for the fully integrated model by invoking a diagrammatic exposition. Let us assume that initially we have balance of payments equilibria so that $B = 0$. Now if we wish to maintain equilibria upon the external account it follows that any worsening of the balance-of-trade account through domestic income expansion must be just offset by an equal improvement in the capital account via the manipulation of interest rate changes. Geometrically, we express this by the payments function in Figure III.1 below which represents the total differential of $B = B(Y, i)$ set equal to zero. We have assumed the function to be non-linear suggesting that there is some critical range of interest rates to which capital movements are especially sensitive. The critical range, indicated by c-c' in the figure, we assume to include the 'average international rate'. The assumption is that below the critical range the raising of the domestic rate has a comparatively minor effect upon the capital account. Once the average rate is approached, however, foreign capital reacts extremely sensitively to minor interest rate

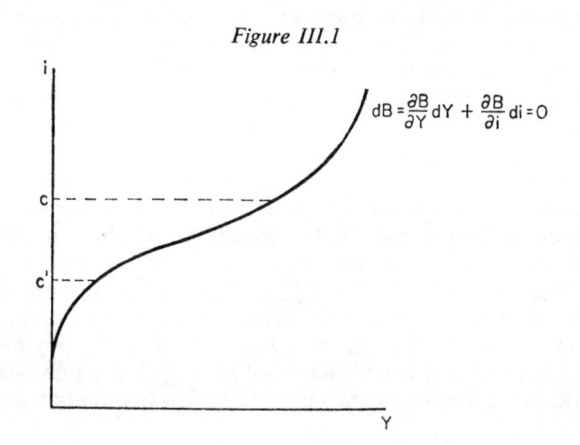

Figure III.1

$$dB = \frac{\partial B}{\partial Y} dY + \frac{\partial B}{\partial i} di = 0$$

changes. Above the critical range, interest-rate increases again have a negligible effect, either because all foreign capital has been absorbed or because the interest rate itself reflects a panic pre-devaluation situation.

Since, for balance of payments equilibria,

$$dB = \frac{\partial B}{\partial Y} \cdot dY + \frac{\partial B}{\partial i} \cdot di = 0$$

then

$$\frac{\partial B}{\partial Y} \cdot dY = - \frac{\partial B}{\partial i} \cdot di$$

and

$$\frac{dY}{di} = - \frac{\partial B/\partial i}{\partial B/\partial Y}$$

which expresses the ratio by which income must be increased to offset a given increase in the interest rate.

For expositional purposes, however, we are currently more interested in the diagrammatic exposition. What we wish to do now is to superimpose the familiar Hicks-Hansen analysis upon Figure III.1.[5] The Hicks-Hansen equation provides us with the simultaneous determination of interest and income, but ignores completely the question of external adjustment. It follows that there is no guarantee that the income and interest levels so determined will be consistent with the balance of payments objective. We illustrate the problem with reference to Figure III.2. We assume initially that the economy is already at full employment—the authorities having successfully manipulated the IS and LM functions to achieve this result—but that a balance of payments deficit exists. In this situation, complete equilibrium will only be achieved by a combined fiscal-monetary policy to offset a decrease in the money stock by increased fiscal spending. Neither monetary policy nor fiscal policy on its own is sufficient to achieve complete equilibrium. The only single instrument policy which can be completely successful in this situation would be devaluation of the currency—reflected in the downward shift of the payments function. Other examples of the combined IS-LM payments adjustment could be given but, quite apart from their purely mechanical nature, we have already demonstrated our basic point. In Chapter II we sought to emphasize the need to consider monetary conditions in evaluating fiscal policy proposals. In the present chapter we have emphasized the need to consider the external sector. A fully comprehensive fiscal policy would take account of both domestic and international money markets, as well as all foreign repercussions and induced income changes. The fiscal policy setting is that of general equilibrium. Whilst it may be conceptually convenient to ignore certain sectors or to adopt simplifying assumptions, it should never be forgotten that we have done so.

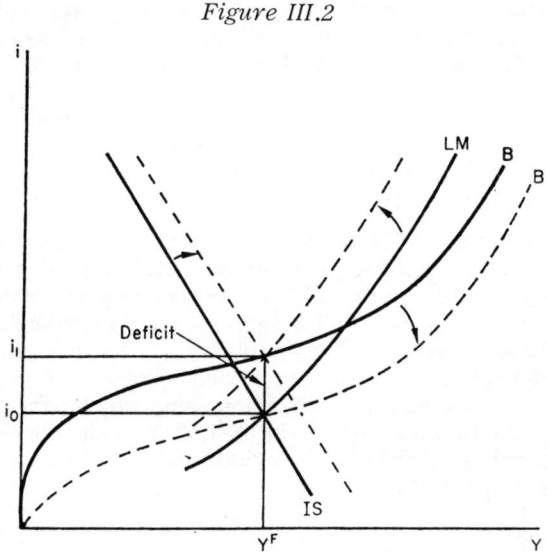

Figure III.2

Initial situation Y^F (full employment income) with interest rate i_0. External deficit represented by i_0-i_1.

Alternative policies:

(a) Restrictive monetary policy plus expansionary fiscal policy to raise interest rates to i_1 at full employment income level.
(b) Devaluation to improve balance of trade and reconcile balance of payments equilibria with full employment at interest rate i_0.

The preceding analysis is very much in keeping with the Keynesian income-expenditure approach to macroeconomic policy which is conveniently summarized in the IS/LM framework. Indeed, it may be contended that the modern theory of fiscal policy is the collective product of numerous manipulations of this simultaneous equation model. It is important to emphasize this point for the model is not without its deficiencies. Being presented in real terms with prices ignored or assumed constant, it does not allow us to analyse the problem of inflation. Nor is it a suitable tool to analyse economic growth since the investment/GNP ratio is masked by the aggregative nature of the IS curve. Moreover, as usually presented—and indeed as presented thus far in the present volume—the IS and LM functions are generally assumed to be independent of each other. Not only is this palpably not the case in the real world but also it is responsible for a false dichotomy's entering into the controversy between the efficacy of monetary versus fiscal control. Finally, the IS/LM analysis is an exercise in comparative statics which ignores both the adjustment path and the time required to move from one equilibrium to another. In policy formulation, these latter considerations may be decisive in the choice of instruments.

Nonetheless, the IS/LM framework offers a convenient expository device in the analysis of policy choice and has proved to be an extremely flexible tool capable of endless modification and adaption.[6] It has shown itself able to incorporate many distinctly post-Keynesian ideas and assumptions into the model analysis without departing from the simultaneous equation framework. Some of the post-Keynesian developments which have influenced the conceptual framework of the IS/LM analysis are indicated below, and they suggest further qualifications to the policy conclusions drawn from the standard model.

V. THE PERMANENT INCOME HYPOTHESIS

Keynesian analysis assumes that both consumption expenditures and the demand for money are functions of recorded or measured income. Influenced by the relatively poor fits obtained from regression analysis alternative hypotheses have been sought, the most influential employing the concept of permanent income. The latter is conventionally portrayed as a geometrically declining weighted average of past and present recorded income.[7] Thus,

$$Y_{pn} = \epsilon Y_n + \epsilon(1-\epsilon)Y_{n-1} \ldots \epsilon(1-\epsilon)^a Y_{n-a} \qquad (III.5)$$

where Y_{pn} denotes permanent income at time period n and a is the number of past income periods relevant in its determination; ϵ is merely the coefficient relating permanent to measured current income. A value of ϵ equal to unity would render the permanent income and Keynesian statements of consumer behaviour identical, whilst a value of zero would imply that current income would exercise no influence whatsoever over current consumption. Consequently, the usual stipulation is $0 < \epsilon < 1$. Let us assume that current consumption, C_n is a function of permanent income, so that

$$C_n = b Y_{pn}$$

It follows that

$$C_n = b(1 - \epsilon) Y_{pn-1} + b\epsilon Y_n$$

which implies that consumption depends upon current measured income plus the permanent income of the preceding period. What are the implications for fiscal policy?

Clearly, tax changes, which are limited in their impact to current income, [8] will now exert less effect upon the level of aggregate demand than they would if consumption were geared solely to measured income. To see this let us consider our original consumption function and examine the consequence of a change in the rate of income tax. Thus,

$$C_n = \alpha + b Y_n (1 - t_y)$$

and

$$\frac{dC_n}{dt_y} = -b Y_n$$

but with our present formulation the impact of the tax change is simply

$$\frac{dC_n}{dt_y} = -b\epsilon Y_n$$

which is clearly less than the above for all b and ϵ less than unity. Once the permanent income concept is invoked the main impact of a fiscal change aimed at altering disposable income is reflected in changes in measured or recorded savings. True, the fiscal change will enter into the determination of future levels of permanent income and thus its effects will be dispersed over an extended time horizon. From the viewpoint of short-term macroeconomic control, however, the reduced potency of tax changes in the current period is a disturbing conclusion for the advocate of fiscal control. Acceptance of the permanent income hypothesis of consumer behaviour would imply a downgrading of the relevance of fiscal policy *per se* in the pursuit of macroeconomic objectives.

However, if consumption is more properly regarded as a function of permanent income, then rationally so too will be the demand for money. Accordingly, modifying our earlier statement (page 21), we can express the demand for money at time period n as

$$L_n = vY_{pn} + \gamma - ci$$

which gives

$$L_n = v(1 - \epsilon)Y_{pn-1} + v\epsilon Y_n + \gamma - ci_n$$

Incorporating these modifications into our generalized IS/LM model we obtain the following sets of equations.[9] From the goods market we now have

$$Y = C + I + G$$
$$C = \alpha + b(1 - \epsilon)Y_{pn-1} + b\epsilon Y^d$$
$$Y^d = Y(1 - t_y)$$
$$I = \beta - qi$$
$$G = \bar{G}$$

which yields

$$Y = \frac{\alpha + b(1 - \epsilon)Y_{pn-1} + \beta - qi + \bar{G}}{1 - b\epsilon + b\epsilon t_y} \qquad (III.6)$$

Thus, permanent income of the preceding period now enters as an argument in the determination of current measured income. From the money market we obtain

$$MS = v(1 - \epsilon)Y_{pn-1} + v\epsilon Y + \gamma - ci$$

which provides the following expression for the rate of interest:

$$i = \frac{v(1 - \epsilon)Y_{pn-1} + v\epsilon Y + \gamma - MS}{c}$$

Again, determination of the interest rate requires knowledge of the permanent income prevailing in the preceding period. Elimination of the interest equation provides the following generalized equation for measured current income:

$$Y = \frac{\alpha + b(1 - \epsilon)Y_{pn-1} + \beta - (q/c)[v(1 - \epsilon)Y_{pn-1} + \gamma - MS] + G}{1 - b\epsilon + b\epsilon t_y + (qv\epsilon/c)}$$

(III.7)

Let us consider, now, the government expenditures multiplier,

$$\frac{\partial Y}{\partial G} = \frac{1}{1 - b\epsilon + b\epsilon t_y + (qv\epsilon/c)}$$

Compare this with the government expenditures multiplier which we derived from our earlier Keynesian analysis,

$$\frac{\partial Y}{\partial G} = \frac{1}{1 - b + bt_y + (qv/c)}$$

Thus, invoking the concept of permanent income, in respect of both consumption and the demand for money, generates an expenditures multiplier which is reduced by the fact that $b\epsilon + b\epsilon t_y < b + bt_y$ but is increased by that $qv\epsilon/c < qv/c$. A priori, we cannot say whether the total impact of the policy change will be greater or less than before although it is clear that if investment expenditure is entirely interest-inelastic (i.e. $q = 0$) then the permanent income expenditures multiplier will always be less than that derived from the simple Keynesian model. Thus whether the impact effect of a shift in government expenditures is reduced by invoking the permanent income hypothesis depends ultimately upon conditions prevailing in the monetary sector.[10]

An alternative way of approaching this question is in terms of the value taken by the coefficient ϵ.[11] A value of ϵ equal to unity renders the permanent income thesis of consumer behaviour identical to the Keynesian formulation. Thus in asking whether the government expenditures multiplier is greater or less in the permanent income case compared to the Keynesian case, one might inquire as to the sign of the cross partial,

$$\frac{\partial^2 Y}{\partial G \partial \epsilon} = \frac{b - bt_y - (qv/c)}{[(1 - b\epsilon + b\epsilon t_y + (qv\epsilon/c)]^2}$$

If this expression were uniformly positive it would mean that a raising of ϵ towards the unity value of the Keynesian model would increase the impact of the government expenditures multiplier, implying that the permanent income hypothesis weakens the efficacy of fiscal intervention. However, there is no clear reason for believing this to be the case. Clearly, the denominator must be positive, as also will the value of $b - bt_y$ in all cases where the tax rate is less than 100 per cent. Whether the latter is sufficient to outweigh the term qv/c must remain open to question although again a perfectly interest-inelastic investment function reduces the term to zero. Thus our conclusion must be that the permanent income hypothesis of consumer behaviour weakens the impact of fiscal action, but when the same analysis is extended to include the demand for money the impact effect of fiscal action could maintain its impact and could even exceed that associated with the simpler Keynesian formulations. Once again we are presented with an example of the dangers inherent in considering fiscal policy independently of monetary repercussions.

VI. WEALTH EFFECTS

Permanent income is a concept closely akin to wealth,[12] and just as fiscal actions may influence permanent income so too it may generate wealth effects which may reinforce or counter its impact. Wealth effects are largely ignored in conventional Keynesian analysis partly because of the tendency to discuss fiscal intervention independently of the budget constraint. We have already touched upon the need to consider the manner in which fiscal policy is financed; we now wish to formulate more precisely the nature of the budget constraint and how different methods of finance may generate opposing wealth effects. In so doing, we will be taking a significant step towards an analysis which illustrates interdependence between IS and LM functions.

The nature of the budget constraint can be indicated in the following way. Total government expenditure less tax receipts in any accounting period must be matched by an equal change in the money supply and/or government securities during the same period. Thus,

$$G + R - T = \Delta MS + \Delta B_g$$

where B_g represents government bonds. Now the significance of the constraint lies in the fact that both money and bonds held by the public will normally be regarded as assets, i.e. as private sector wealth. It follows that any expenditure change not matched by tax changes will generate wealth effects in the private sector which will either reinforce or offset the fiscal impact.

Let us consider, first of all, an increase in government expenditures financed by an increase in the money supply—outside money to the private sector. If consumption is geared to net private sector wealth, the increase in monetary wealth generates expenditure changes which reinforce the initial spending change by the government. In terms of the conventional IS/LM model, the outward shift of the IS function stemming from the fiscal change is reinforced, not only by an equivalent outward shift of the LM curve as the money supply expands, but also by an additional shift of the IS curve owing to induced consumption effects. Nor need this be the end of the story. Since both the IS and LM curves experience outward shifts it is possible for the interest rate to fall, which will be reflected in the increased market value of government bonds so generating further expansionary wealth effects on consumption spending. True, there will be some offsetting inward movement of the LM curve if the demand for money is also a function of monetary wealth, but there can be no denying the overall conclusion that increased expenditure financed by increased money supply has a powerful impact upon the macroeconomy. There seems little point in arguing whether the fiscal or the monetary action is the more potent force; it is surely the policy mix which should be evaluated as a whole and not its constituent parts.

The more interesting—and far more complex— case concerns an expenditure change financed by the issue of new government securities. Let us assume both consumption and the demand for money to be positive functions of private sector wealth, W, where the latter is taken to include both money and government bonds. Thus, $W = MS + B_g$ where B_g refers to the outstanding value of government securities. For simplicity, at least for the moment, we ignore price changes. This permits us to equate any increase in private sector bond holdings with an increase in private wealth.[13] We may now invoke the previous model, replacing permanent income by private wealth, to obtain

$$Y = \frac{\alpha + b(1-\epsilon)(MS + B_g) + \beta - (q/c)[v(1-\epsilon)(MS + B_g) + \gamma - MS] + G}{1 - b\epsilon + b\epsilon t_y + (qv\epsilon/c)}$$

(III.8)

It follows that if we have combined change in government spending financed by increased bond issue we are evaluating

$$\frac{\partial Y}{\partial G} \cdot dG + \frac{\partial Y}{\partial B_g} \cdot dB_g$$

where $dG = dB_g$ to obtain

$$dY = \left[\frac{1}{1 - b\epsilon + b\epsilon t_y + (qv\epsilon/c)}\right]dG + \left[\frac{b - \epsilon b - (qv/c) + (qv\epsilon/c)}{1 - b + b\epsilon t_y + (qv\epsilon/c)}\right]dG$$

$$= \left[\frac{1 + b - \epsilon b - (qv/c) + (qv\epsilon/c)}{1 - b + bt_y + (qv/c)}\right]dG \gtrless 0$$

Clearly, the expression may be positive or negative. The first part of the numerator will certainly be positive, summarizing the expansionary effects of government expenditure plus the induced impact upon consumption as bondholding is increased. Yet, equally, the latter part of the numerator is negative, as $qv\epsilon/c < qv/c$, and thus the total outcome must remain unknown. Diagrammatically, what is described is the outward shift of the IS function as it is offset by the inward shift of the LM curve, consequent upon the increased demand for money holdings as private wealth is increased. The net impact must remain in doubt; it is conceptually possible for the fiscal action to be entirely negated.

It is partly for these reasons that monetarists have remained sceptical about the impact of fiscal intervention in the absence of monetary expansion and have criticized the 'Keynesian' school for concentrating only upon the initial impact—the outward shift of the IS curve—and ignoring induced reactions upon the LM curve. Certainly, a strong case can be made out for the need specifically to consider wealth effects and thus to dispense with the assumption of independence between IS and LM functions. Nonetheless, the foregoing analysis clearly overstates the strength of the wealth effect in that it assumes rigidity in the price of government bonds. In fact, however, the only means the government will have of inducing greater bondholding by the public is to make the interest yield more attractive—i.e. to decrease the price of existing bonds. Clearly, a negative wealth effect must be implied for existing bondholders which offsets in part the increase in the nominal holding of bonds. In this connection it may be noted that the analysis is not perfectly symmetrical. In the case of the government's financing expenditures by issuing new bonds, existing bondholders suffer a capital loss—even if unrealized. The purchasers of the new bonds do not obtain any corresponding capital gain; they merely give up cash in return for income-yielding securities. In contrast, if the government cuts expenditure and uses the money saved to retire part of the existing debt, those induced to part with the debt will experience a capital gain in real terms whilst those continuing to hold bonds will experience a similar if unrealizable capital gain. Does this not imply stronger wealth effects for contractionary as opposed to expansionary shifts in government expenditure functions?

When prices are allowed to vary the analysis is rendered extremely complex, for now what matters is not the outstanding volume of bonds or their par value but their current marketable value which is intimately linked with methods of government finance. Moreover, our scepticism of the wealth effect is reinforced, since expansionary increases in government spending will most probably be accompanied by increases in the general price index whilst the issue of new bonds will imply a fall in existing bond prices. On both counts the wealth effect is severely weakened. Finally, it should be recalled that the alleged wealth effect springs from a form of 'debt illusion', for the ultimate redemption of the debt carries with it a future tax liability equal to its nominal value. Considerations such as these do much to reinforce the claims of fiscal policy even in the absence of accompanying monetary expansion.

VII. DISPOSABLE INCOME AND THE DEMAND FOR MONEY

In our discussion of permanent income and wealth effects we have adopted the same behavioural assumptions with respect to the demand for money as we did in regard to consumer outlays. Logically, this procedure seems perfectly rational, for if the public is motivated by certain considerations in respect to goods then surely the same considerations should apply to its demands for money which is, after all, a good yielding utility like any other.

In the earliest Keynesian formulations consumption was related directly to GNP. Later more sophisticated versions, still in keeping with the Keynesian tradition, related consumer expenditure to disposable income and indeed that is the practice we have followed in this volume. The question is immediately raised: why should the demand for money not also depend on disposable income? [14]

If this procedure is adopted then once more the counter-cyclical claims of fiscal policy are called into question, for now a tax increase moving the IS curve inwards will be accompanied by a fall in the demand for money, generating an outward shift of the LM curve and countering the fiscal action. Conceptually, a positive tax multiplier is a possible outcome. This conclusion can be readily seen if we make the transactions demand for cash read

$$L^t = vY(1 - t_y)$$

This is sufficient to generate from the money market the LM equation

$$i = \frac{vY - vYt_y + \gamma - MS}{c}$$

which when combined with our usual IS statement yields, for the equilibrium level of national income,

$$Y = \frac{\alpha + \beta - (q/c)(\gamma - MS) + \bar{G}}{1 - b + bt_y + (qv/c) - (qvt_y/c)} \qquad \text{(III.9)}$$

Accordingly, our tax multiplier is now

$$\frac{dY}{dt_y} = \frac{[-b + (qv/c)][\alpha + \beta - (q/c)(\gamma - MS) + \bar{G}]}{[1 - b + bt_y + (qv/c) - (qvt_y/c)]^2}$$

If investment is highly interest-elastic, implying a high value for q, then it is possible for $dY/dt_y > 0$. The rationale for this result is simply that the decline in disposable income induced by the tax change reduces the demand for money, generating a fall in the rate of interest. If investment demands are sufficiently responsive to a decline in the interest rate the increase in investment demands may more than offset the fiscal change. Once again we

VIII. THE ACCELERATOR PRINCIPLE

The accelerator, by which investment demands are related to changes in income or consumption, possesses a long history dating as far back as at least 1917, when J. B. Clark made it an explicit part of his celebrated *The Economics of Overhead Costs*. Yet despite this it played no part in the economics of the *General Theory*, unless it is to be inferred from the influence of expectations upon investment and the implication that expectations may be geared to recent consumer demands. It has been, of course, a comparatively simple matter to introduce the accelerator into Keynesian analysis with the expected result of magnifying the multiplier and hence the impact of fiscal change. Let us consider, for example, the following model.

From the goods market we have

$$Y = C + I + G$$
$$C = \alpha + bY^d$$
$$Y^d = Y(1 - t_y)$$
$$I = \beta - qi + \Omega Y$$
$$G = \bar{G}$$

where the only change has been to relate investment demand to income as well as to the rate of interest. This provides us with the IS curve,

$$Y = \frac{\alpha + \beta - qi + \bar{G}}{1 - b + bt_y - \Omega}$$

Combining with our usual LM equation,

$$i = \frac{vY + \gamma - MS}{c}$$

allows us to solve for Y. Thus,

$$Y = \frac{\alpha + \beta - (q/c)(\gamma - MS) + \bar{G}}{1 - b + bt_y - \Omega + (qv/c)}$$

and the government expenditures multiplier is now

$$\frac{dY}{dG} = \frac{1}{1 - b + bt_y - \Omega + (qv/c)}$$

which is greater than before owing to the inclusion of $-\Omega$ in the denominator.

An interesting consequence of relating investment to income is that it is made perfectly possible for the IS curve to have a positive slope. This will indeed occur if, in the present model, the marginal propensity to invest exceeds the marginal propensity to non-consume gross income, i.e. when $\Omega > 1 - b + bt_y$. Consider the IS equation obtained above. This may be rewritten as

$$Y = \frac{\alpha + \beta + \bar{G}}{1 - b + bt_y - \Omega} - \frac{q}{1 - b + bt_y - \Omega} \cdot i$$

and its slope is given by $-q/(1 - b + bt_y - \Omega)$. Since q is positive, the IS curve will possess a positive slope only when the donominator is negative.

While it is interesting to speculate upon the nature of positively sloped IS curves and their implications for policy, the consequences seem more profound for monetary than fiscal action.[15] There are also delicate questions raised concerning the stability of any indicated equilibrium.[16]

Clearly we have by no means exhausted the numerous qualifications and modifications one can make to the basic IS/LM analysis and doubtless the student with a facility for model building will discover others for himself. In each case the implications for monetary and fiscal policy will differ and in some cases will differ significantly. In the last resort, the relevance of fiscal action to macroeconomic control will depend upon future empirical findings. On this point there will surely be agreement between monetarists and 'neo-Keynesians'.

NOTES

[1] Providing of course that the marginal importing propensity of country B exceeds zero and tax rates are less than 100 per cent.
[2] k_a being greater than 1 for all $0 < b_a, t_{ya}, j_a < 1$.
[3] The European Economic Community has in fact emphasized the need

(4) For the following proof we are greatly indebted to Professor Robert W. Kilpatrick of Cornell University.
(5) For the precise manner in which the IS/LM diagram is derived for an open economy see either Dwayne Wrightsman, 'IS, LM and External Equilibrium: A Graphical Analysis', *American Economic Review*, March 1970, or Robert M. Stern, *The Balance of Payments: Theory and Economic Policy*, Aldine Treatises in Economics, Macmillan, London, 1973, Ch. X.
(6) Our extension of the IS/LM analysis to the open economy provides a fitting example of its ease of manipulation.
(7) Cf. Milton Friedman, 'The Demand for Money: Some Theoretical and Empirical Results', *Journal of Political Economy*, Aug. 1959.
(8) Tax changes will, of course, influence the level of future permanent income, but they cannot influence past levels of permanent income. Conceptually, we may think of past levels of permanent income being net of tax.
(9) To simplify the notation, all variables refer to the current time period n, unless it is specifically stated otherwise.
(10) Cf. D. E. W. Laidler, 'The Permanent Income Concept in a Macroeconomic Model', *Oxford Economic Papers*, March 1968, and 'Expectations, Adjustment and the Dynamic Response of Income to Policy Changes', *Journal of Money, Credit and Banking*, Feb. 1973.
(11) Cf. M. T. Sumner, 'Fiscal Policy and the Permanent-Income Hypothesis', *The Manchester School*, December 1974.
(12) Permanent income being the present discounted value of all anticipated income *flows*, wealth being a current *stock* of monetary and non-monetary assets. Where the latter is defined to include human capital the analogy becomes closer still.
(13) The money stock, of course, remains unchanged. Whilst the public gives up cash to acquire new bonds it is replenished by the government expenditure.
(14) This issue was first raised by J. M. Holmes and D. J. Smyth in 'The Specification of the Demand for Money and the Tax Multiplier', *Journal of Political Economy*, Jan./Feb. 1972.
(15) With a positively sloped IS curve monetary expansion serves to raise the equilibrium rate of interest, thus benefiting the capital account of the balance of payments and offsetting in part the decline in the balance of trade induced by income expansion. For this and related argument see William Silber, 'Monetary Policy Effectiveness: the Case of a Positively Sloped IS Curve' *Journal of Finance*, Dec. 1971, and Paul Burrows, 'The Upward Sloping IS Curve and the Control of Income and the Balance of Payments', *Journal of Finance*, June 1974.
(16) The stability condition being that the slope of the IS curve is less than that of the LM curve.

Chapter IV

FISCAL POLICY, EMPLOYMENT AND THE PRICE LEVEL

I. INTRODUCTION

In the previous analysis, stabilization policy has been taken to mean the exercise of control over the level of national expenditure (or aggregate demand) and over the balance of payments, i.e. the attainment of specific values of Y and $X - M + B^K$. However, this definition of stabilization is hardly satisfactory. What stabilization means to politicians and to the ordinary public is control over employment conditions and over the general price level, for these factors have the most direct economic influence on community well-being. (For the moment we do not consider the community interest in achieving a satisfactory level of economic growth.) An examination of contemporary policy discussion in developed countries would confirm that one of the main themes is the problem of combining high and stable levels of employment with a stable or gently rising price level. We consider this important problem of 'trade-off' between these two objectives or stabilization policy in Section III below, but for the moment it is clearly important to investigate how we can extend our analysis to trace the connexion between changes in aggregate demand and changes in output, employment and prices.

A simple way of showing the link can now be demonstrated. Let us assume that the economy consists of a large number of identical firms interested in maximizing profits. This enables us to consider conditions in one firm as representative of production relations in the whole economy.

The profit-maximizing condition of the firm is

$$P_j = \frac{w}{f'(N_j)} \qquad (\text{IV.1a})$$

or

$$\frac{w}{P_j} = f'(N_j) \qquad (\text{IV.1b})$$

where P_j = market price of the product of the jth firm

w = wage rate (taken as given)

$f'(N_j)$ = marginal product of labour, N_j being the volume of employment in the jth firm.

The fraction of total revenue paid to wage-earners is defined as wN_j/P_jQ_j, i.e. as the total wage bill divided by the total revenue, Q_j being the quantity of product produced by the jth firm. Now we multiply both sides of equation IV.1b by N_j/Q_j, i.e. the reciprocal of the average product of labour, and we have

$$\frac{wN_j}{P_jQ_j} = \frac{f'(N_j)}{Q_j} \cdot N_j \qquad (IV.2a)$$

Calling N_j^a the average product of labour ($= Q_j/N_j$), then rearranging terms gives us

$$\frac{P_jQ_j}{wN_j} = \frac{N_j^a}{f'(N_j)} \qquad (IV.2b)$$

For the whole economy this may be written as

$$\frac{PQ}{wN} = \sum_{j=1}^{n} \frac{P_jQ_j}{wN_j} = \sum_{j=1}^{n} \frac{N_j^a}{f'(N_j)} \qquad (IV.3)$$

where PQ is the total revenue of n industries.

For simplicity, let us drop the subscript j and, ignoring summation terms, represent the situation in the whole economy as

$$\frac{PQ}{Nw} = \frac{N^a}{f'(N)}$$

It follows from this expression that the level of employment is a function of aggregate demand, the ratio of marginal product to average product of labour, and the wage rate, for

$$N = PQ \cdot \frac{f'(N)}{N^a} \cdot \frac{1}{w} \qquad (IV.4)$$

In rather *simpliste* Keynesian models, it is often assumed that changes in aggregate demand, and therefore in output, do not alter the general price level, that the marginal product of labour is equal to or greater than the average product, and that the wage rate remains constant up to the full-employment level. Making $P = 1$ and $f'(N) = N^a$, and treating $1/w$ as a constant, say ϵ, then

$$N = Q\epsilon$$

and therefore

$$\frac{dN}{dQ} = \epsilon \qquad (IV.5)$$

Employment then becomes a linear function of the value of output equal to the value of national income, both at constant prices for $P = 1$. Further, if we still assume a constant price level, we can define the value of real output as equal to national expenditure in the following way:

$$Q \equiv C + I + G \qquad (IV.6)$$

where all components are measured in real terms and the price level remains constant for any *changes in values* of all components. Given I and G as autonomous, consumption as a linear function of national income after tax, and the only tax as a proportional tax on income, t_y, we have

$$Q = \frac{1 + G}{1 - b(1 - t_y)}$$

It follows from equation IV.5 that

$$\frac{\partial N}{\partial G} = \left[\frac{1}{1 - b(1 - t_y)} \right] \epsilon \qquad (IV.7)$$

The expression in square brackets in equation IV.7 is an 'employment multiplier' whose value depends on the consumption coefficient and the tax rate. Noting the restrictive assumptions already listed, the corollary to our analysis must be that the more flexible are the price level and the wage rate, the more tenuous is the relationship between budgetary changes and the level of employment.

A review of the analysis so far indicates that if the price level, P, is to be affected by budgetary action, it will only be brought about through changes in aggregate demand, e.g. by raising G in the manner frequently described. So far, however, we have made no reference to the possibility of using taxes on expenditure, e.g. sales taxation, as a fiscal control, and this omission can be conveniently rectified at this juncture.[1]

Consider an *ad valorem* tax on consumption goods. The imposition of such a tax as an addition to the fiscal armoury will clearly have effects similar (but not identical) to those of raising an equal yield of income taxes by a rise in tax rates. If it is assumed, for example, that community spending does not alter in money terms, producers of the taxed goods will receive less than total expenditure by the amount of the consumption tax 'take'. In consequence, wages and profits will be cut back and, following this, private incomes and subsequently private consumption will fall. At less-than-full employment levels, output and employment are likely to fall and, depending on the shape of firms' marginal cost curves, prices as well. At the same time, one form of protection for producers will be to recoup their falling receipts by raising prices in response to the tax, the extent to which they will do so depending on the elasticities of demand for and supply of their product. This suggests a counter-influence on the direction of price change, although it would be difficult to offer a prediction of the final effect on the general price level without a more detailed analysis of the tax-shifting process.

We now introduce a tax on consumption, t_i, reckoned for analytical convenience as part of the buyer's price. The wage rate, w, is taken as given. Our profit-maximizing condition, as found in equation IV.1, has now to be modified as follows, in order to take account of the fact that the price per unit to the firm is now the market price *less* the price per unit multiplied by the tax rate, i.e.

$$P(1 - t_i) = \frac{w}{f'(N)} \text{ or } P = \frac{w}{f'(N)} \cdot \frac{1}{(1 - t_i)} \qquad (\text{IV}.8)$$

We have now identified some of the ingredients which will compose a revised model of the economy which clearly distinguishes income, output, employment and prices. In addition, we have identified a new tool of fiscal policy—a tax on consumption. At this stage we can now proceed to examine the properties of this model and how far it modifies or extends previous conclusions about the effects of changes in fiscal instruments.

II. A SIMPLE MODEL COMPARING THE EFFECTS OF AN INCOME TAX AND CONSUMPTION TAX ON OUTPUT, EMPLOYMENT AND PRICES

Recalling equation IV.6 we define the real national product in a closed economy as

$$Q \equiv C + I + G$$

where C is real consumption by households, and I and G are investment and government expenditure on goods and services respectively, both measured in real terms. We assume the two latter to be independent of changes in income. We also assume that there are no transfer payments.

Money national product at market prices, Y, is given by

$$Y = CP^c + (I + G)P^k \qquad\qquad (IV.9)$$

where P^c is the price of consumption goods and P^k the price of 'capital goods' (including government purchases). If the index numbers of P^c and P^k are both chosen to equal 100 when the tax on consumption goods, t_i, is zero, and if the price of consumption goods is marked up by the amount of the tax[2], then

$$P^k = (1 - t_i)P^c$$

Hence money national product at factor cost, Y_f^m, is

$$Y_f^m = CP^c(1 - t_i) + (I + G)P^k = (C + I + G)P^k = QP^k \qquad (IV.10)$$

and disposable income, Y^d, is

$$Y^d = (1 - t_y)Y_f^m = (1 - t_y)QP^k = (1 - t_y)(1 - t_i)QP^c$$

where t_y is the proportional income-tax rate.

Let us assume that consumers do not suffer from 'money illusion', i.e. they take account of tax-induced price changes when taking consumption decisions. Then

$$C = \alpha + (bY^d/P^c) = \alpha + b(1 - t_y)(1 - t_i)Q \qquad (\text{IV. 11})$$

Substituting the consumption function into equation IV. 6, we have

$$Q = \frac{\alpha + I + G}{1 - b(1 - t_i)(1 - t_y)} \qquad (\text{IV. 12})$$

Inspection of equation IV. 12 reveals that both taxes appear in the multiplier. Accordingly, it is not possible to make any definite statement about the comparative effects of a change in the rate of income tax *vis-à-vis* a change in the rate of consumption tax since the net effect in each case will depend upon the other rate of tax. More formally, we have

$$\frac{\partial Q}{\partial t_i} = \frac{-(b - bt_y)(\alpha + I + G)}{[1 - b(1 - t_i)(1 - t_y)]^2}$$

and

$$\frac{\partial Q}{\partial t_y} = \frac{-(b - bt_i)(\alpha + I + G)}{[1 - b(1 - t_i)(1 - t_y)]^2}$$

It follows that the consumption tax multiplier will be negative provided the income tax rate is less than 100 per cent, whilst the income tax multiplier will be negative as long as the consumption tax rate is less than 100 per cent. A raising of the rate of income tax weakens the impact of a consumption tax change and vice versa; alternatively, the existence of an income tax acts as an automatic stabilizer against consumption-tax-induced disturbance, whilst the existence of a consumption tax serves equally as an automatic offset to the impact of an income tax change. This is brought out by consideration of the cross partials, both of which are positive, i.e.

$$\partial^2 Q/\partial t_i \partial t_y > 0 \text{ and } \partial^2 Q/\partial t_y \partial t_i > 0.$$

In passing, it may be noted that this situation creates problems for the assessment of the effectiveness of fiscal measures. A fiscal change may exert a relatively weak impact owing to the existence of extremely efficient automatic fiscal stabilizers elsewhere. Would one consider the fiscal system to be more effective in the absence of such stabilizers, reinforcing the impact effect of fiscal action but simultaneously rendering it more susceptible to autonomous disturbance?

Although, *a priori*, we cannot reach any qualitative conclusion concerning the comparative impacts of an income tax *rate* change and a consumption tax *rate* change, it is possible to say something about the comparative deflationary impact of these taxes when they are expressed in terms of fiscal yield.[3] Conventionally, the comparison is made by comparing the yield of a consumption tax required to effect a given decrease in income, with income taxes zero, with the yield of an income tax required to effect the same income decrease, with sales taxes zero.

With direct taxes the yield is

$$T_y = t_y Q P^k$$

With a consumption tax the yield is

$$T_i = t_i C P^c = t_i [b(1-t) + bQ] P^k$$

on substituting from equations IV.10 and IV.11. It can be shown[4] that, given the 'normal' Keynesian assumption that the marginal propensity to consume is less than unity, then it requires a greater tax yield to reduce Q to some given level if one uses a direct tax rather than a consumption tax, and so, conversely, a given tax yield will have a greater 'deflationary impact' if levied in the form of a consumption tax. The intuitive explanation is obvious: even if a consumption tax does not lead to a substitution effect in favour of savings, its impact per pound of yield is greater because all the tax is at the expense of consumption rather than some of it serves merely to replace private by public saving. Pound for pound, therefore, a consumption tax is found to be 'more deflationary' than an income tax.

This conclusion, however, rests on a special set of assumptions which we have examined in Section I of this chapter. Imagine a situation in which the economy is at the full-employment level, and the expectation is that *ex ante* aggregate demand will exceed *ex ante* aggregate supply which is constant. With no policy intervention, and using a *simpliste* Keynesian model which ignores the monetary system, there would be a rise in prices, without a concomitant rise in employment and output. As we have demonstrated, we can cut aggregate demand by either an income tax or a consumption tax in order to prevent the price rise, but whereas a lower yield of consumption tax is necessary to achieve the given downward movement in aggregate demand, the consumption tax only achieves this result by a *once-and-for-all price rise*! This must follow from the analysis because the consumption tax is only able to bring about the cut in consumption if it is passed forward in higher prices.

Even if one accepts that a rise in the consumption tax rate would result in price rises lower than those which would otherwise obtain without any adjustment in tax rates, and ignores the 'double-think' surrounding the proposition that a consumption tax is 'more deflationary' although it produces a price rise, we must clearly look more closely at the effects on the analysis of relaxing the special assumptions mentioned on p. 70. It will be remembered that these assumptions enabled the simple Keynesian analysis to dispense with the consideration of the maximizing behaviour of firms and individuals, and to avoid considering what happens if there is a 'trade-off' between employment and price changes. In addition, the model does not allow any investigation of 'cost-push' inflation or the wage-price spiral, which empirical investigations have indicated as important.

The next section of this chapter attempts to combine some of the elements in Sections I and II of this chapter, but the reader is warned that one cannot take account of all the additional complications mentioned in the previous paragraph. All we can hope to do, given the constraint of space and the level of analysis of this volume, is to demonstrate in what direction modern economic analysis must move in order to examine in depth the link between output, employment, prices and the control of their movements by fiscal policy.

III. AN EXTENSION OF THE SIMPLE MODEL

It may be useful to begin by setting up our full set of equations for the extended model, before considering each one:

$$N = N(Q) \qquad \text{(IV. 13a)}$$

$$P^c = \frac{w}{f'(N)} \cdot \frac{1}{(1 - t_i)} \qquad \text{(IV. 13b)}$$

$$Q = C + I + G \qquad \text{(IV.13c)}$$

and by assuming that we adopt the assumption of no money illusion in the consumption function

$$Q = \frac{\alpha + I + G}{1 - b(1 - t_i)(1 - t_y)} \qquad \begin{array}{l}\text{(IV.14)}\\(= \text{IV.12})\end{array}$$

Equation IV.13a is a revised version of equation IV.5, but we remove the strong assumption that employment is a linear function of national output. We shall assume that $dN/dQ > 0$ and $d^2N/dQ^2 < 0$. Equation IV.13b is simply the alternative version of equation IV.8. It will be assumed initially that the wage rate, w, is constant. It is further assumed that we are interested only in movements in the price of consumption goods, these being the only goods subject to the *ad valorem* tax of rate t_i. In equations IV.13c and IV.14, I is exogenously determined.

Let us now consider what the effect will be on output, employment and the price level of a change in either income tax or consumption tax, and let it be assumed that policy demands that a given change in Q is needed. If this is so, we know from previous analysis that the amount of the consumption tax needed to produce a given fall in Q is less than the amount of income tax. As Q changes by a given amount, the consequential fall in employment is the same in both cases. However, as employment will fall more rapidly than output, then the marginal product of labour will rise. This means that, with no other changes in the independent variables in equation IV.13b, P^c must fall, given the profit maximization condition already considered in Section I, which led to the formulation in equation IV.8. However, this fall in P^c is only consistent with the case in which we use a change in t_y, i.e. in the rate of income tax, in order to reduce Q. If we use the alternative of a rise in t_i, then clearly the price-reducing effect of the rise in labour's marginal product is offset by the rise in t_i. Whether or not P^c will rise will depend on the exact shape of the marginal product curve of labour and, of course, on the change in t_i. For any given change in t_i, the closer the marginal is to the average product of labour—as commonly found in Keynesian-type models—the greater is the likelihood of a rise in P^c.

Having proceeded this far in modifying the Keynesian analysis of income determination in order to take account of the effects of different taxes on the level of employment, output, and prices, one is tempted, like Pandora, to open the box of hidden assumptions which, once allowed to escape, destroy the simple innocence of the model presented. If we are brave enough to do this, then there are at least two major problems confronting us.

The first is whether or not it is reasonable to assume that any change in P^c will leave the level of real aggregate demand unaffected. Let us rewrite the multiplicand in equation IV. 14 so that $\alpha + I + G = Z$. In terms of our analysis, can we assume that $dZ/dP^c = 0$? There is a whole host of reasons why one may question this assumption. It would be dangerous to assume that, on balance, $dZ/dP^c = 0$. On the whole, one might hazard the guess that real aggregate demand is likely, if anything, to decrease, *other things being equal*, if P^c rises and vice versa if P^c falls. Consider the following four factors:

(i) *Distribution effects.* If it is assumed that money aggregate demand remains constant but P^c rises, then with a constant wage rate and a fall in employment there will be a redistribution of income from wages to profits (cf. equation IV. 2a). The normal conclusion would be that such a redistribution, if it did not alter the value of Z, would lower the value of b in equation IV. 14, so that real consumption demand would fall.

(ii) *Money supply exogenously determined.* Unless the supply of money is demand-determined, i.e. will respond automatically to changes in money aggregate demand, a price increase will tend to reduce the liquidity of the economy, leading to higher interest rates. As we know from the analysis in Chapter II this may curtail spending.

(iii) *Substitution effects of the tax.* Whereas the assumption in the consumption function employed in equations IV. 11 and IV. 14 postulates that the consumer will raise his consumption out of a given income in order to allow for the cut in its real value by the consumption tax, other assumptions are possible. There could be a 'money illusion' in the consumption function, which would mean that consumers only maintain the money value of consumption despite the raising of prices by the consumption tax. Our consumption function has now to be rewritten as

$$CP^c = \alpha + b(Y^d) = \alpha + b(1 - t_y)(1 - t_i)QP^c$$

or

$$C = (\alpha/P^c) + b\,(1 - t_y)(1 - t_i)Q \qquad\text{(IV. 10a)}$$

Equation IV. 12 has now to be rewritten as

$$Q = \frac{(\alpha/P^C) + I + G}{1 - b(1 - t_y)(1 - t_i)} \qquad \text{(IV. 12a)}$$

In short, a price increase caused by the consumption tax would reduce the constant term in the consumption function, and I and G could also decline if firms' and government demand were fixed in terms of the money and not the real value of services.

(iv) *Balance of trade effect.* If prices of consumption goods rise relative to the price of competing imports, and the exchange rate is fixed, demand may be switched to purchases from foreign buyers, thus reducing real demand at home.

The foregoing considerations reinforce the underlying contention that consumption taxes are more deflationary, pound for pound, than income taxes, even though they generate a once and for all price increase. However, thus far we have explicitly assumed that wage rates remain constant even in the face of rising consumer prices. The plausibility of this assumption must be questioned, for trade unions rationally will bargain for a real wage and will respond to any rise in the price index of consumption goods. That is to say, with no change in the overall bargaining position of those concerned, the wage demand will be expressed as

$$\frac{W_{n+1}}{P^C_{n+1}} = \frac{W_n}{P^C_n}$$

where n denotes the time period involved. The prospect of a wage-price spiral set off by a tax change which altered prices might transform our conclusion about the comparative deflationary impacts of direct and indirect taxes.[5] The issue is by no means clear-cut, however, for equally it may be contended that trade unions respond to changes in direct taxation and bargain for a given 'take-home pay' expressed in real terms.[6] The wage demand would then be expressed (again assuming no change in the overall bargaining position) as

$$\frac{W_{n+1}(1 - t_{y_{n+1}})}{P^C_{n+1}} = \frac{W_n(1 - t_{y_n})}{P^C_n}$$

Is there any reason to assume that the wage-price spiral will differ for an income tax as opposed to a sales tax if wage earners negotiate to maintain a real command over consumption goods? Although the sales tax will exert an initial price effect (absent in the case of the income tax) which will feed back upon wage demands and thus initiate the wage-price spiral, the income tax will be responsible for a larger initial compensatory wage claim which will feed back upon prices. The larger compensatory wage claim is a direct result of the fact that the income tax requires a greater fiscal yield than the sales tax to attain the same real deflationary impact. Clearly, in the last resort the question is an empirical one to be resolved by reference to the available evidence.[7] There seems little doubt, however, that the experience of inflation and its consequence of pushing wage earners into higher marginal tax brackets has conditioned trade union negotiators to be as acutely aware of the direct tax burden as they are of the retail price index.

To build a wage-price spiral into our model, set off by a tax change which altered wages or prices, would require two major alterations in the model's structure. In the first place, it would be necessary to 'dynamize' the model and show the period-by-period changes in the variables which interest us. Our model only portrays the conditions which produce static equilibrium in the commodity market and the labour market and equilibrium is assumed to be achieved instantaneously. Unfortunately, dynamizing such models would take us far beyond the analytical scope of this work.[8] The second major alteration would be in the nature of the assumptions about economic policy. We have examined the effects only of alternative tax changes without specific reference to policy 'mixes'. Only later do we consider what happens when we build in assumptions about the *desirability* of the changes produced in output, employment and prices by fiscal action. To sustain a wage-price spiral, we would have to build in the assumption that trade unions in pressing for higher wages could reasonably expect that the 'cost' of doing so would not be an increase in unemployment of its members and therefore that employers also could reasonably hope to pass wage claims forward. In other words, offsetting adjustments would be made in variables controlled by government, e.g. the money supply, to accommodate wage earners and employers.

To conclude, therefore, the extension of the 'normal' Keynesian-type expenditure model to examine changes in variables other than aggregate demand is a complicated business, and the reader must accept that we have only been able to scratch the surface of many of the problems encountered in approaching greater realism. At the same time, it seems better to let him know that these difficulties exist, even if they are not surmounted, rather than to lead him astray into believing that movements in aggregate demand offer enough information about the direction of movements in prices, wages, employment and output, as the more naive Keynesian models would have us believe.

NOTES

(1) Despite the fact that taxes on expenditure often comprise 50 per cent or more of the total tax 'take' in many countries, their place in the economic analysis of fiscal policy is often forgotten about. A partial explanation lies in some of the difficulties of introducing such taxes into conventional macroeconomic analysis, which will be manifest in the analysis which follows.

(2) The reader familiar with tax shifting theory will realize that this is a strong assumption if compatible with profit maximization by all firms. This assumption is commonly used in Keynesian fiscal policy models: but see Section III of this Chapter.

(3) See, for example, E. Cary Brown, 'Analysis of Consumption Taxes in Terms of the Theory of Income Determination', *American Economic Review,* March 1950, and R. A. Musgrave, *The Theory of Public Finance,* McGraw-Hill, New York, 1959, pp 447-52.

(4) Hence $T_y > T_i$ if
$$t_y Q P^k > t_i [b(1-t) + bQ] P^k$$
i.e. if $(1-b)(1-t)Q > b$.
Private saving, S, is given by disposable income minus expenditure on consumption. With $t_i = 0$, we have
$$S = (1 - t_y) Q P^k - C P^k$$
$$= (1-b)(1-t_y) Q P^k - b P^k$$
on substituting from IV.11 and IV.12. With $t_y = 0$ we have
$$S = Q P^k - C P^c$$
$$= \frac{[(1-b)(1-t_i)Q - b] P^k}{1 - t_i}$$

In both cases it is evident that the condition for private savings to be positive is $(1-b)(1-t)Q > b$, which is the same as the condition for $T_y > T_i$.

(5) For an example of an attempt to extend the analysis in this direction, see A. T. Peacock and J. Williamson, 'Consumption Taxes and Compensatory Finance', *Economic Journal,* Vol. LXXVII, March 1967. Most of this section is based on this article.

(6) See, for example, D. A. L. Auld, 'The Impact of Taxes on Wages and Price', *National Tax Journal,* March 1974.

(7) The question remains an empirical one because, whilst it is possible to incorporate such wage demand equations in formal models, in the final analysis the result will depend upon the degree to which employers concede such tax-induced demands.

(8) Cf. the attempt made in A. T. Peacock and J. Williamson, *op. cit.*

Chapter V

FISCAL POLICY AND ECONOMIC GROWTH

I. INTRODUCTION

By extending the analysis to the sphere of economic growth, we are taking an essential step towards attaining greater realism and relevance for fiscal policy, for conclusions derived from static analysis may no longer be applicable when we permit dynamic considerations. [1] Regrettably, however, it must be conceded that the theory of fiscal policy within a dynamic setting is still very much in its infancy. Whilst much has been done in assessing the impact of tax changes upon investment incentives, saving ratios, work effort and so forth—all factors which may influence growth rates—comparatively little has been done to bring fiscal changes more formally into growth models. There appear to be two major reasons for this. Firstly, most of the policy discussion has been concerned with specific fiscal proposals designed to influence actual short-term growth rates, whereas the greater part of growth theorizing has been concerned not with actual growth rates as such but rather with the required rates needed to fulfil certain long-term conditions. It can hardly be considered surprising if the economic policy maker should feel somewhat remote from the concern with golden-age solutions. Secondly, and possibly of more importance, it is also the consequence of the fact that recent growth theory has developed in such a way as to render fiscal considerations virtually irrelevant to long-term growth paths. This latter development has been associated with the gradual eclipse of the Harrod-Domar model in favour of neo-classical formulations. In the former case growth rates are almost entirely determined by capital formation and fiscal policy consequently has a major role to play. [2] In the neo-classical formulations, however, growth rates are wholly determined by population growth; fiscal policy may indeed be used to hasten capital formation but this results only in a changed capital–labour ratio and exerts no impact upon the long-term growth path. Fiscal policy thus becomes an irrelevancy. [3]

Whilst we will critically examine this conclusion at a later stage, it remains a fact that from the practical standpoint of policy-making the existing theoretical framework of economic growth does not contribute substantially to fiscal policy. Nor is it easy to adapt the above models in order to apply them to the relevant policy issues in public finance. We are thus compelled to discuss fiscal policy for economic growth in a context which is largely divorced from the theoretical framework of growth economics. Indeed, this is one of the major contrasts between dynamic and static fiscal policy. In the latter case the static theory of fiscal policy is a logical extension of static Keynesian theory, whereas fiscal policy for economic growth has yet to find its theoretical foundation.

II. HARROD-DOMAR GROWTH

When the Harrod-Domar model is extended to the government sector the increase in capacity income will be a function of both private investment spending and also government spending where the latter is utilized to enlarge capacity output.[4] We shall assume that the increase in capacity output in the current period n, is determined solely by the total amount of investment spending in the previous period. Thus we may write

$$\Delta Y_n^C = h(I_{n-1} + p G_{n-1})$$

where Y^C denotes capacity income, the subscript n the time period involved, and p the percentage of government expenditure which is essentially of an investment character. h is the output–capital ratio which we here assume to be identical between the government and private sectors. Whilst this assumption may appear to be a little tenuous at first glance it is as well to note that conceptually we can always render the output-capital ratio equal between the sectors by making the corresponding adjustment in p.

Turning to the demand side of the economy, we adopt a simple Keynesian national income model expressed in monetary terms and have

$$Y_n^m \equiv C_n^m + I_n^m + G_n^m$$

where the superscript m denotes the monetary unit. Consumption we assume to be a simple function of disposable income in the current period and we make the simplifying assumption that average and marginal propensities are equal. Thus, $C_n^m =$

$bY_n^m(1-t_y)$ where t_y is the rate of income tax and assumed invariant. Thus, $t_y = T_n^m/Y_n^m$ where T is the tax yield. Following Domar we take investment expenditures to be autonomously determined [5] and finally we make government expenditures a constant proportion of national income so that

$$I_n^m = I_{n-1}^m = \bar{I}_n^m$$

$$G_n^m = gY_n^m$$

Accordingly, the equilibrium level of money national income is

$$Y_n^m = \frac{\bar{I}_n^m}{1-b+bt_y-g}$$

and the increase in aggregate demand resulting from an increase in the level of investment spending is

$$\Delta Y_n^m = \frac{\Delta I_n^m}{1-b+bt_y-g}$$

If it is assumed that full employment prevails initially, continued full employment of the capital stock without inflation requires that the increase in monetary demand just matches the increase in capacity income. Thus the required condition is that

$$\Delta Y_n^c = \Delta Y_n^m$$

or, alternatively,

$$h(I_{n-1} + pG_{n-1}) = \frac{\Delta I_n^m}{1-b+bt_y-g}$$

Dividing throughout by Y_{n-1}^m we obtain

$$\frac{\Delta Y_n^m}{Y_{n-1}^m} = \frac{hI_{n-1}}{Y_{n-1}^m} + \frac{hpG_{n-1}}{Y_{n-1}^m} = \frac{\Delta I_n^m/(1-b+bt_y-g)}{I_{n-1}^m/(1-b+bt_y-g)}$$

But since $G_{n-1}/Y_{n-1}^m = g$, and I_{n-1}/Y_{n-1}^m is simply $1-b+bt_y-g$, we may express our required condition as

$$\frac{\Delta Y_n^m}{Y_{n-1}^m} = h(1-b+bt_y-g+pg) = \frac{\Delta I_n^m}{I_{n-1}^m}$$

This equation postulates that the required growth of monetary aggregate demand, needed to maintain full employment of the capital stock, is equal to the required growth of monetary investment expenditures and, moreover, is itself a function of both government spending and tax changes. It follows that, if the actual growth of income falls below the required, it is possible to do one of two things: either to attempt to raise the actual growth rate by a programme of investment incentives and the like, or alternatively to decrease the required growth of income by the manipulation of taxes and expenditures. Of the two, the former policy of raising actual growth rates is possibly preferable from a welfare viewpoint but perhaps also the more difficult, for, if actual growth rates lag behind the required, then excess capacity must exist and attempts to increase investment spending are hardly likely to succeed. Accordingly, it would seem more appropriate to examine the implications of varying taxes and government spending so as to influence the required rate of growth, Y^r.

An increase in the rate of taxation will raise the required rate of growth since $dY^r/dt_y = hb$ and is positive in all cases where the marginal propensity to consume is positive. Likewise, an increase in the level of government spending—assuming that p remains unaltered—will normally reduce the required rate of growth since $dY^r/dg = h(p - 1)$ and is negative in all cases where p is less than one. More interesting, perhaps, is the case of a balanced budget change.

We want to evaluate

$$\frac{\partial Y^r}{\partial t_y} \cdot dt_y + \frac{\partial Y^r}{\partial g} \cdot dg$$

where $dt_y = dg$. Thus we have

$$(hb)dg + h(p - 1)dg$$

The resulting impact upon the required rate of growth is determined solely by the extent to which government expenditures are capacity-creating. If $p = 1$, so that there is no consumption element in government expenditures, then the balanced budget change reduces to $(hb)dg$ and is positive in all cases where the marginal propensity to consume is positive. Similarly, if $p = 0$, so that all government spending is of the nature of consumption, then the impact of a balanced budget change reduces to $(hb - h)dg$ and the required growth rate must fall. It follows that there is some value of p such as to leave the required growth rate unaffected. Our conclusion must be that, given a discrepancy between required and actual growth rates, variations in taxes and expenditures may achieve equality between the two by influencing the required growth rate. Other examples could be invoked. However, whilst of some pedagogic value in illustrating the implications of the Harrod-Domar model, it is hardly likely that the results will be of direct relevance to fiscal policy. For our concern—and indeed Harrod and Domar's initial concern—is not limited solely to attaining full employment of the capital stock. Of greater importance, perhaps, is the need to secure the full employment of the labour force. The assumption that one can equate full employment of the capital stock with full employment of the labour force is a convenient one often invoked, but not one likely to enhance the status of the economics profession. Should the labour force be expanding at a faster rate than the actual growth of income, a policy of decreasing the required growth of income is tantamount to adopting a policy of perpetual unemployment. Clearly, in this situation, the need is for specific measures to raise the actual growth rate in the endeavour to attain a 'golden age' solution where actual rates, required rates and population rates are brought into equality. Regrettably, the Harrod-Domar formulation offers little in the way of a solution to this question. Our conclusion must be that from the pragmatic standpoint of fiscal policy the Harrod-Domar model offers little that is relevant.

III. THE NEO-CLASSICAL MODEL

Whilst the Harrod-Domar formulation of the growth process was undoubtedly an important conceptual extension of the Keynesian model, in retrospect it seems clear that the peculiar characteristics of the analysis sprang from the limiting and certainly questionable assumption of fixed-factor proportions. The alternative assumption, that the capital-labour ratio is variable, is the essential distinguishing feature of the neo-classical model. It follows, again in contrast to the Harrod-Domar model, that the capital-output ratio is also variable. Both these postulates rest upon a second assumption, often only implicitly stated, that entrepreneurs react to changes in comparative factor prices. If capital is expanding faster than the labour supply, for example, the rate of interest falls relative to wages and entrepreneurs are induced to adopt more capital-intensive methods. More often than not, such a behaviouristic assumption is incorporated into the analysis by invoking the mathematically convenient Cobb-Douglas production function. Now, it is clear that such a production function will minimize the role of fiscal policy, for, whilst taxes can be manipulated to increase total saving, the employment of greater capital-intensive methods of production will be accompanied by a decline in the marginal product of capital. Indeed, the fundamental conclusion of the neo-classical model is that the long-run growth rate of the economy is determined uniquely by the growth rate of population, and accordingly, fiscal policy is of no consequence. [6] In what follows we will first of all examine a neo-classical growth model to derive this basic result. [7] We will, however, examine the implications for fiscal policy in somewhat more detail. We may find that the scope for fiscal policy is rather less limited than hitherto supposed.

National income is assumed to consist of homogeneous commodities whose growth, ΔY, is assumed a simple function of time. Of any increment in income, a fraction, s, is saved, being immediately invested and the remainder consumed. Thus, we may write $s = S/Y = I/Y$, and $1 - s = C/Y$. Capital accumulation is the consequence of net investment over time. Net investment may therefore be defined as the growth of the capital stock with respect to time. Accordingly we have $I = sY = dK/dn = \dot{K}$ where K represents the capital stock. We now assume a production function of the following form, $Y = E(K, N)$ where N represents the labour input. It is convenient to assume that the production function is of the Cobb-Douglas variety implying constant returns to scale and diminishing returns to the input of any one factor. We also assume that labour input is growing at a constant rate, ψ, so that

$$N(n) = N_0 e^{\psi n}$$

where ψ is the growth rate of the population. We now have

$$\dot{K} = sY = sE(K, N) = sE(K, N_0 e^{\psi n})$$

This is a differential equation the solution of which determines the time path of capital accumulation which must be followed if all the available labour input is to be fully employed, given the nature of the production function and the saving propensity, s.

The next step is to introduce the notion of the capital-labour ratio, r, which, in sharp contrast to the Harrod-Domar model, is explicitly introduced as a variable. The fundamental assumption of the model is that changes in relative factor prices—determined by the marginal productivity doctrine—will ensure that full employment of both labour and capital is maintained. Given this basic assumption, which as we have already indicated implies an assumption about entrepreneurial behaviour, then the purpose of the neo-classical model is to show that no matter what the rate of growth of the labour force may be, there is always a time path of capital accumulation consistent with its full employment.

The capital-labour ratio, r, is of course K/N. The proportionate rate of change with respect to time in r, therefore, is simply equal to the proportionate rate of change in K minus the proportionate rate of change in the labour force. Hence we have

$$\frac{\dot{r}}{r} = \frac{\dot{K}}{K} - \frac{\dot{N}}{N}$$

But $\dot{N}/N$ is simply the growth rate of population, ψ, and we already have $\dot{K} = sE(K, N)$. Thus we may write

$$\dot{r} = r \cdot \frac{sE(K, N)}{K} - \psi r$$

We can now make use of the assumption of a Cobb-Douglas production function. Since this exhibits constant returns to scale, it is possible to divide both factors K and N by N, providing we multiply the total function by the same amount. Thus

$$\dot{r} = r \cdot \frac{sNE\left(\frac{K}{N}\right)1}{K} - \psi r$$

But $K/N = r$, so $N/K = 1/r$ and the total expression reduces to

$$\dot{r} = sE(r, 1) - \psi r$$

This equation is of fundamental importance to the argument which follows. It may be interpreted in the following way: $E(r, 1)$ is simply the total output of one worker which varies according to the amount of capital at his disposal. It is thus output per capita as a function of capital per capita. Likewise, $sE(r, 1)$ may be considered as the amount of saving per capita expressed as a function of capital per capita. ψr may be considered as the proportionate change in the capital-labour ratio with respect to time as a consequence of population growth.

Thus the total expression,

$$\dot{r} = sE(r,1) - \psi r$$

gives the rate of change in the capital-labour ratio as a function of the increase in savings per worker due to income growth and the decrease in capital per worker due to population growth.

Clearly, three situations are possible. Two cases are: (a) if $\dot{r} > 0$, it implies that the increase in capital per worker due to income growth exceeds the decrease occasioned by population expansion; and (b) conversely, if $\dot{r} < 0$, the capital-output ratio is declining as a consequence of population expansion's running ahead of net capital formation. The dividing case (c) is represented by $\dot{r} = 0$, where the increased capital formation arising from income expansion is exactly offset by the force of population expansion thus maintaining the capital-labour ratio as a constant. It is precisely this case which provides the long-term equilibrium solution to the neo-classical framework. It is inherent in the neo-classical construct that whatever the initial value for $\dot{r}$ it will converge towards zero. To see this, consider the implications of $\dot{r} = 0$. If $\dot{r} > 0$ then the amount of capital per worker is increasing. But, given the assumption of a Cobb-Douglas production function, the increasing capital input will be subject to progressively diminishing returns. National income will continue to grow, but at an ever-decreasing rate. With a constant savings ratio, it follows that savings will also continue to grow but at an ever-decreasing rate. Meanwhile population continues to expand at an exogenously determined rate. Thus, although initially savings were outstripping the growth of population, leading to a rising capital-labour ratio, the combination of a declining rate of change in savings growth together with a constant rate of change in population growth must inevitably lead to a situation at which the respective growth rates coincide. At this point the volume of savings is just sufficient to maintain the newly discovered capital-labour ratio. Similar reasoning applies to the opposite situation should $\dot{r} < 0$. Thus ultimately $\dot{r}$ approaches zero and the capital-labour ratio remains constant. With a constant amount of capital per capita, the production function then determines the level of income per capita. If income per capita is thus rendered a constant, it follows that the growth rate of the economy as a whole must be exactly in line with the growth rate of population. It is in this sense that we may say that, in the neoclassical model, the rate of growth is determined uniquely by the growth rate of population. Thus, no matter what rate of population growth we may initially assume, the required adjustment in the savings ratio will occur providing a time path of capital accumulation consistent with the maintenance of full employment.

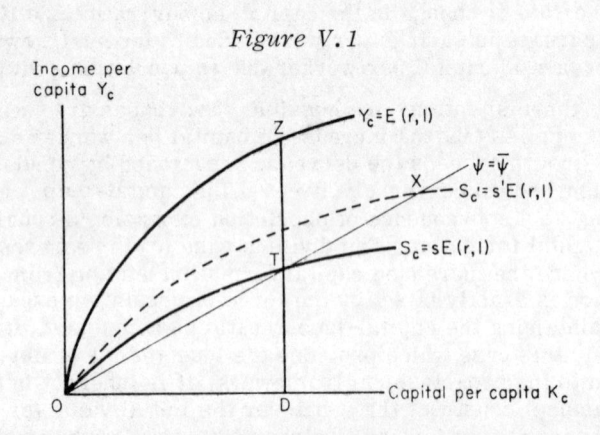

Figure V.1

The essence of the argument may be summarized diagrammatically. [8] In Figure V.1, income per capita is measured along the vertical axis and capital per capita along the horizontal. The production function, summarized by the term $E(r, 1)$, then denotes the path of income per capita as a function of capital per capita. Since we are assuming that the production function is linear homogeneous, it passes through the origin; it is positively inclined but at a diminishing rate owing to the operation of diminishing returns. Thus

$$\frac{d}{dK_c}(E, 1) > 0 \text{ and } \frac{d^2}{dK_c^2}(E, 1) < 0$$

Since we are assuming that the savings ratio is a constant, the savings function, $sE(r, 1)$, which denotes the amount of saving per capita as a function of income per capita will be a replica of the production function. The vertical distance between the production function and the savings function measures the amount of consumption per capita as a positive function of capital per capita.

Finally, since population growth is exogenously determined, its constant growth rate ψ is indicated by the slope of the population function $\psi = \bar{\psi}$.

In Figure V.1 equilibrium is found at T where the rate of savings growth is just equal to the growth rate of population. The capital-labour ratio is thus maintained as a constant equal to OD. With this amount of capital per capita, the production function determines income per capita equal to DZ. Consumption per capita is represented by ZT and saving per capita by DT. The capital-output ratio is simply OD : DZ. Since all these magnitudes are constants and expressed in per capita terms, the economy in the aggregate must be growing in accordance with the growth of population, ψ. It may be noted that no other solution offers a stable equilibrium. At levels of capital per capita in excess of OD, for example, the rate of population growth exceeds the rate of capital accumulation and the capital-labour ratio cannot be maintained. It must fall back towards OD. Likewise, should the initial position imply a capital-labour ratio less than OD the growth of the capital stock exceeds the growth of population. Profit-maximizing behaviour and flexibility in comparative factor prices will lead to a raising of the capital-labour ratio towards OD. The position OD, therefore, corresponds to the convergence of $\dot{r}$ towards zero.

IV. THE SCOPE FOR FISCAL POLICY

If we accept the implications of the model—and it should be emphasized that the model followed here is a highly simplified one-sector, one-commodity model of the growth process—does any function remain for fiscal policy? At first glance the answer is unmistakably no. Taxation may be used to modify the savings function so that $S = I = sY(1 - t_y)$ where t_y is the effective average rate of income tax. If the government utilizes the proceeds for direct investment then our savings function becomes

$$S = I = sY(1 - t_y) + t_y Y$$

Alternatively, the government may use part of the proceeds in consumption expenditure and part in investment activities whence the savings equation is given by

$$S = I = sY(1 - t_y) + pt_y Y$$

where p is the percentage of government revenues which are of a capacity-creating character. Hence the introduction of a government sector may either increase or decrease the total volume of savings for any given income level according to the value of p. However, such a complication can easily be accommodated by making the corresponding adjustment in s. If we denote s' to represent the savings ratio after tax and expenditure changes, then conceptually the equation

$$\dot{r} = s'E(r,1) - \psi r$$

provides us with a solution similar to before. Although the equilibrium capital-labour ratio will be altered $\dot{r}$ will again converge on zero. The capital-labour ratio will again be a constant, implying a constant per capita income, and the growth of the economy will again be equated with the growth rate of population. Since this is exogenously determined, and presumably unaffected by fiscal policy, the government's tax and expenditure measures have no impact upon the long-term rate of growth.

Diagrammatically, this situation is portrayed in Figure V.1. We assume that government fiscal policy has been responsible for a raising of the savings ratio indicated by the broken curve,

$$S'_C = s'E(r,1)$$

The equilibrium position will be shifted to position X, implying a higher capital-labour ratio which in turn implies a higher per capita income, but the aggregate expansion of the economy continues to be ψ once the new equilibrium has been attained. The inescapable conclusion appears to be that fiscal policy is powerless to influence the overall growth rate.

Even if we were to accept this conclusion—and the reader may be warned that we have no intention of so doing—it does not necessarily imply that fiscal policy has no role to play. Indeed, the role of fiscal policy may well be vital. For, even though fiscal measures may leave the growth rate unaffected, they will certainly influence the volume of consumption. In the recent emphasis upon economic growth and the desirability or otherwise of raising growth rates, it seems to have been forgotten that one fundamental aim of economic endeavour is consumption. Enhanced growth is desirable only to the extent that it permits greater consumption at some future date—and only then if the future consumption streams have been adequately discounted.

It should be noted that we are not even concerned with raising income per capita as such, except in so far as it permits greater consumption. It is consumption, and not income, which is the index of economic well-being.[9] It follows that if the growth rate of the economy is determined solely by population growth, then the government may utilize fiscal policy to influence the savings ratio in the direction of maximum consumption.

Our problem then reduces to a simple one in constrained maximization. Since consumption per capita is simply

$$C_c = Y_c - S_c = E(r, 1) - sE(r, 1)$$

we wish to maximize this subject to the constraint that

$$sE(r, 1) - \psi r = 0$$

The constraint ensures that we satisfy the stability condition that $\dot{r} = 0$. The economic meaning of satisfying this condition may be interpreted as follows. Fiscal policy measures can be varied so as to select that capital-labour ratio which maximizes consumption per capita as long as the volume of saving then forthcoming is just sufficient to equip the expanding labour force with an identical amount of capital.

We form the function,

$$\Pi = E(r, 1) - sE(r, 1) + \lambda[sE(r, 1) - \psi r]$$

where λ is the undetermined Lagrange multiplier. If the partials are set to zero with respect to r, s and λ, solving the resulting equations provides us with the necessary conditions for maximizing consumption:

$$\Pi_r = \frac{\partial}{\partial r}[E(r, 1)] - \frac{\partial}{\partial r}[sE(r, 1)] + \lambda \cdot \frac{\partial}{\partial r}[sE(r, 1) - \psi r] = 0$$

$$\Pi_s = \frac{\partial}{\partial s}[-sE(r, 1)] + \lambda \cdot \frac{\partial}{\partial s}[sE(r, 1) - \psi r] = 0$$

$$\Pi_\lambda = \frac{\partial}{\partial \lambda}[sE(r, 1) - \psi r] = 0$$

Figure V.2

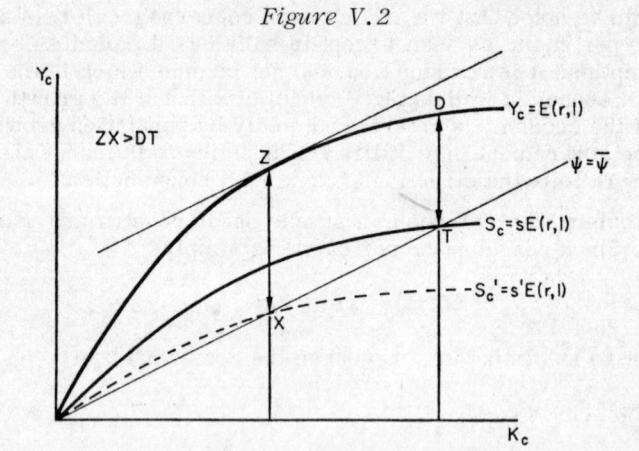

In Figure V.2 the condition for maximizing consumption is attained at position X, where the slope of the production function equals the slope of the population function so that

$$\frac{d}{dK_C}[E(r,1)] = \frac{d\psi}{dK_C} \text{ and } \frac{d^2}{dK_C^2}[E(r,1)] - \frac{d^2\psi}{dK_C^2} < 0$$

It follows that, if the initial equilibrium position was T, then fiscal policy should be employed not merely to diminish the savings ratio but also to decrease the level of income per capita! Moreover, within the confines of the present model it should be noted that this conclusion is quite independent of the time horizon of the community's indifference curve. Consideration of future generations in no way modifies the policy conclusion that the existing degree of capital accumulation exceeds that which is optimal. Clearly fiscal policy has a major role to play even if we concede that growth rates are exogenously determined.

Other considerations present themselves. Let us assume that an autonomous shift in the saving propensity occurs so as to raise the proportion saved out of any given level of income. According to the model, a new equilibrium will be found at a higher capital-labour ratio. But this conclusion implies a behavioural assumption upon the part of entrepreneurs. The tacit assumption must be that the increase in capital formation lowers the cost of capital investment and induces more capital-intensive modes of production. A Keynesian floor to interest rates or interest-inelastic investment demand functions will prevent the required adjustment being made. The situation corresponds to the Harrod-Domar case where the labour force is expanding less rapidly than the growth of income required to maintain full employment of the capital stock. Excess capacity is the outcome. In the neo-classical formulation with the more conventional assumption of Cobb-Douglas production functions, this situation is prevented by increases in the capital-labour ratio. But, as we have already suggested, such an adjustment may be prevented—hence the need for fiscal changes to provide the incentive to adopt more capital-intensive methods.

Even if the adjustment process does take place of its own accord, the time interval required may be such as to invite fiscal intervention. Recent theoretical work upon this point has suggested that fiscal policy can appreciably shorten the adjustment period.[10] If this be the case, then it follows that active compensatory policy may indeed be essential to ensure that the 'golden age solution' is attained within a time period deemed acceptable by policy-making bodies.

Thus far we have explicitly accepted the neo-classical contention that the growth rate is determined uniquely by the rate of population growth. It is now time to challenge this underlying postulate. The element which has been ignored is that of technological change. The model hitherto presented has assumed implicitly that technological progress is zero. If technological change is allowed to enter the analysis, as realistically it should, then the rate of population growth ceases to be the sole determinant of growth. If technological progress responds to fiscal incentives, then fiscal policy becomes a joint determinant of the growth process.

Now, there is a considerable body of opinion which leans towards the viewpoint that technological change is embodied within the act of investment. Increasing the rate of investment thus hastens the pace of technological advance. If this is the case—and it should be emphasized that this issue is still a controversial one[11] —fiscal policy which raises the investment—GNP ratio is also the vehicle of technical change. Technical progress is revealed in the parametric upward shift of the production function raising the level of per capita income associated with any given capital-labour ratio. It follows, given the assumption of a constant saving propensity, that it also occasions a similar parametric upward shift of the savings function which in turn will generate a new equilibrium corresponding to a higher capital-labour ratio. But, in the process, the attempt to equip each member of the labour force with a larger volume of capital equipment may generate new technological change and reinforce the cycle. Indeed, there is no reason to assume that stable equilibria will ever be regained, for the impact of technological progress may always counter diminishing returns so as to generate increased savings at a higher rate than population growth. This type of situation is portrayed in Figure V.3. Again we assume an initial equilibria

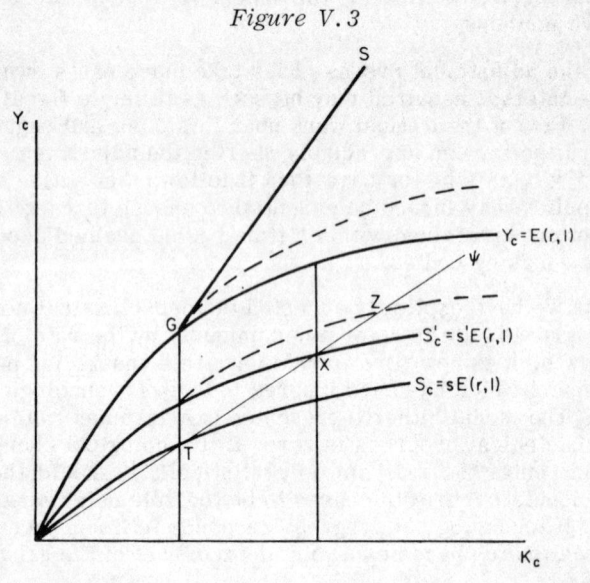

Figure V.3

at T and consider the impact of fiscal policy to raise the savings ratio. In the absence of technological change the new equilibria would be indicated at X—fiscal policy would have attained a once-and-for-all change in per capita income without influencing the growth rate. Now, however, we assume that the new investment needed to raise the capital-labour ratio incorporates a degree of technical progress. Both the production function and the savings function are shifted upwards—as indicated by the broken curves—and a new equilibrium is again indicated at Z. But Z need never be attained. Investment-induced technology may again occur and the upward shift of the production function be made continuous. In this case the economy is moving along a long-term growth path such as GS with per capita income continually rising. The growth rate of the economy always exceeds that of population growth, ψ.

The present analysis, where a once-and-for-all fiscal change takes the economy to the point where technological innovation becomes self-sustaining, is clearly related to the Rostovian economics of the take-off. At low levels of capital per worker, technological progress is inhibited; a certain capital intensity is required before innovation can occur. The task of fiscal policy is to force an increase in savings to transform existing methods of production and attain the required capital intensity. The difficulty faced by so many less-developed countries is how to pursue such a policy when faced with surplus labour resources and the consequent need to adopt labour-intensive methods for full employment.

The foregoing has indicated the importance of introducing technological progress into the neo-classical growth model. Policy measures to induce investment are again of significance in the growth process if such investment embodies technological progress. In recent years the belief that investment is the key to advanced economic growth has led to a series of policy proposals designed to stimulate investment by the private sector. One of these proposals which has received wide endorsement—the so-called strict fiscal-easy money policy for economic growth—will be critically examined in a later chapter in the present work. For the moment, however, it is sufficient to note that we can relate policy proposals directly to the conceptual framework of growth theory. If this is not the case—if policies for economic growth are completely divorced from theoretical considerations—then either the theory or the policy, or both, must be held deficient.

Before the present chapter is concluded it will be illuminating to apply the present model to an issue of particular importance to the less advanced economies, namely that of population growth. Our theoretical framework has adopted the simplifying assumption that population growth is exogenously determined and expanding at a constant rate, ψ. In terms of a developed industrial economy, such an assumption appears perfectly tenable. Below a certain level of per capita income, however, population growth may be more properly regarded as a function of per capita income. Below subsistence income population growth will, by definition, be negative. As income per capita rises above subsistence it is reasonable to assume that population growth responds rapidly as death rates fall. Once death rates have stabilized, the rate of population growth is likely to decline to a more 'normal' level and then become relatively insensitive to further income growth. A variable population growth raises many issues which are portrayed in Figure V.4.[12] In the diagram, no less than three possible intersections occur between the savings and population functions. Of these, points A and C may be regarded as stable equilibria in the sense that any small disturbance will be self-correcting as $\dot{r}$ approaches zero. In contrast, equilibrium at B is unstable and any minor disturbance is perpetuated. If the economy is initially at position A, it is caught in an unenviable low-level trap with low per capita income and consumption. Piecemeal attempts to raise the investment ratio will be self-defeating; the economy will return to A. What is required is a major fiscal effort, possibly accompanied by international aid, to raise capital per capita beyond the level indicated by B. If this is attained the economy will propel itself to the comparatively high consumption and income level C. The argument may be reinforced if we assume position B to denote the capital-labour ratio at which investment-induced technological change becomes self-sustaining.

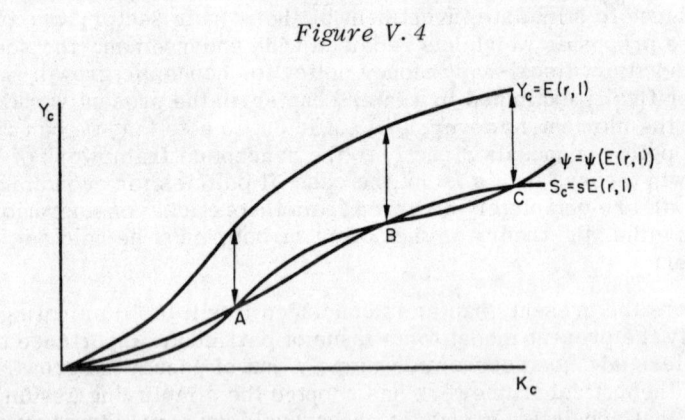

Figure V.4

Y_c axis, K_c axis; curves $Y_c = E(r,l)$, $\psi = \psi(E(r,l))$, $S_c = sE(r,l)$; intersections at A, B, C.

The reader need hardly be reminded that the models employed in the present chapter are extremely simplified. As a basis for practical policy discussion they can provide no more than an elementary conceptual framework pertinent to the issues of growth economics. Nonetheless, it is clear that fiscal parameters have their place in such models—and not least in the neoclassical construct.

NOTES

(1) It may be shown, for example, that automatic fiscal stabilizers may actually be destabilizing when considered in a dynamic setting! Cf. D. J. Smyth, 'Can Automatic Stabilizers Be Destabilizing', *Public Finance*, 1963, and A. T. Peacock, 'Built-in Flexibility and Economic Growth' in Gottfried Bombach (ed.), *Stabile Preise in Wachsender Wirtschaft*, Tübingen, 1960. We will return to this issue in Chapter VI.

(2) This approach, the essence of which is the assumption of a constant capital-output ratio, is still very much in favour in discussions concerning the less advanced economies.

(3) Fiscal policy parameters have indeed been included in neo-classical growth models by a number of authors in recent years. For the most part, however, they have been concerned with distributional issues, or with the speed of adjustment to the growth path given any autonomous disturbance—and not with the underlying nature of the growth path itself. Cf. J. Cornwall, 'Three Paths to Full Employment Growth', *Quarterly Review of Economics*, Feb. 1963; R. Sato, 'Fiscal Policy in a Neo-Classical Growth Model', *Review of Economic Studies*, Feb. 1963; and K. Sato, 'Taxation and Neo-Classical Growth', *Public Finance*, No. 3, 1967.

(4) Cf. R. A. Musgrave, *The Theory of Public Finance*, McGraw-Hill, New York, 1959, pp. 484 ff.

(5) In Harrod's formulation an attempt is made to relate investment spending to income changes by invoking the accelerator principle. We will have recourse to this additional sophistication when we consider the Harrod-Domar model and automatic stabilization. See Chapter VI.

(6) Even within the confines of the neo-classical framework, this conclusion may be a little too sweeping. Growth rates are of course determined by the growth of the labour force and not by the growth of population. It is perfectly possible that fiscal policy variables may influence participation rates, for example.

(7) The simple model presented here follows closely the pioneering article by R. M. Solow, 'A Contribution to the Theory of Economic Growth', *Quarterly Journal of Economics*, Feb. 1956.

(8) The presentation here follows that of H. G. Johnson, 'The Neo-Classical One-Sector Growth Model: A Geometric Exposition and Extension to a Monetary Economy', *Economica*, Aug. 1966.

(9) Although, of course, savings may be viewed as a consumption good which enters into the individual's utility function.

(10) The reference here is to an unpublished manuscript by Douglas Dosser, 'Adjustment through Fiscal Policy in Neo-Classical Growth Models'. The starting point for this discussion will be found in R. Sato, 'Fiscal Policy in a Neo-Classical Growth Model: An Analysis

of Time Required for Equilibrating Adjustment', *Review of Economic Studies*, Feb.1963, and K. Sato, 'On the Adjustment Time in Neo-Classical Growth Models', *Review of Economic Studies*, July 1966.

(11) The rationale for believing that net investment incorporates technical progress is the empirically observed fact that investment activity is seldom mere replacement investment. Usually, the newly acquired capital asset is considered superior to the one which it replaces—witness the remarkable progress in computers, for example. The difficult empirical question, however, fundamental to policy, is whether technical change is an increasing or diminishing function of the rate of investment.

(12) Other complexities can be introduced by making the savings propensity also variable with income per capita. In the present analysis this complication is ignored. It may be noted that *a priori* the impact upon the savings propensity is by no means clear. On the one hand the savings ratio might be expected to increase with rising income. A corollary of the model, however, is that rising income per capita is accompanied by higher capital-labour ratios and hence a lower comparative return to capital accumulation. Logically, interest rates should fall.

Chapter VI

STABILIZATION POLICY IN A DYNAMIC SETTING

I. INTRODUCTION

The foregoing analysis has been expressed within the framework of comparative static methodology. We have focused upon a given equilibrium condition and then analysed the impact of a once-and-for-all change—e.g. a fiscal policy change—in moving the economy to a new equilibrium. Our concern is then limited to comparing the two equilibrium states in order to gauge the efficacy of fiscal action. It follows that we are not concerned with the time period of adjustment *per se*; implicitly we have assumed the adjustment period to be instantaneous. As an expositional device, such an assumption has the great virtue of simplifying macroeconomic relationships; the desired values of policy objectives are held constant and the actual values adjusted to them simply by the application of policy instruments. Since the adjustment period is infinitely small, neither desired nor actual values may change of their own accord; the advantage of comparative static methodology is that the system is insulated against extraneous shocks. Our attention may be focused solely upon the declared objective and the policy tools at our disposal, and the complexities of changing variables in the real world ignored.

Whilst pedagogically justified, in the realm of practical decision-making such a procedure is clearly faced with difficulties. Apart from the logical inconsistency inherent in assuming a time period so short that nothing can alter—save for those variables we wish to change—for policy purposes the time period of adjustment may be of vital importance. Indeed the choice between using one policy instrument as compared with another may depend upon the time interval required. As we have already indicated, the selection of available policy tools involves a comparative cost-benefit evaluation in which the time element is but one of the factors to be taken into account. In the present chapter, we wish to show the importance of time for stabilization policy. Our basic conclusion is that, once time periods are assumed finite, stabilization policy is rendered much more difficult and may even work in a perverse manner—a result of considerable importance to the issue of discretionary versus automatic stabilization policy. [1]

II. A SIMPLIFIED VIEW OF THE DYNAMICS OF FISCAL POLICY

Before we proceed with the formal analysis, a simple example may serve to outline the essence of the argument. Let us assume that both the desired and actual levels of GNP are a function of time—the former being equated with the desired growth of income compatible with full employment and the latter being a cyclical movement around the long-term desired trend. When the actual level of GNP exceeds the desired level, an inflationary situation is indicated, and when the actual falls short of the desired level, resources are unemployed. Conventional fiscal and monetary policy would indicate a restrictive policy in the former case and expansionary measures in the latter, in order to equate actual and desired income levels. Suppose, however, that a time interval must elapse before the intended policy measures can take effect; in this case it is possible for restrictive monetary and fiscal policy to exert its influence when the economy has already moved into recession of its own accord, or conversely it is possible for expansionary policies to exert their impact when the normal cyclical movements of income are already culminating in an inflationary boom. In this case, illustrated in Figure VI.1, stabilization policy serves as a positive destabilizer magnifying the normal movements of the trade cycle.

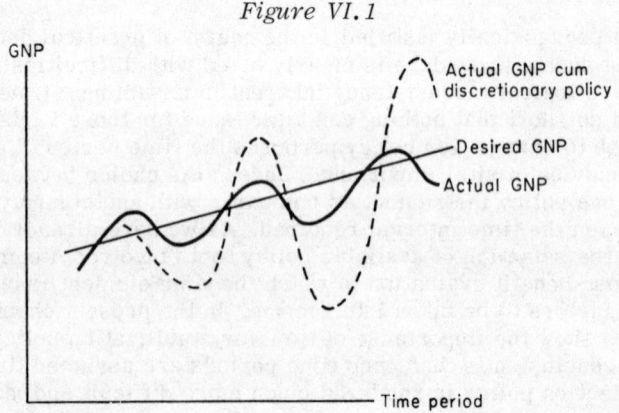

Figure VI.1

It remains to enquire as to the reasons for the delayed impact of discretionary fiscal and monetary policy. First of all, time is required before the policy maker can be certain that corrective action is needed. Data are seldom current; a three-month lag in the availability of statistics is often the best that can be expected. Time is also required for analysis; indices of economic activity frequently offer conflicting evidence and underlying trends may be obscured by seasonal influences. Thus, by the time the policy maker is convinced of the need to intervene to correct destabilizing movement of income, such a movement may have already reversed itself. Secondly, major changes in discretionary policy may require legislative approval which may not be readily forthcoming, and the subsequent public debate may contain announcement effects which of themselves exert destabilizing influences. Finally, there is the time needed for proposed measures to take effect which will depend in part upon the differing response patterns of the taxpayer and the banking public.

It is this delayed impact of discretionary stabilization measures—which as we have seen may imply perverse destabilizing consequences—which has led to the call for the abandonment of attempts at discretionary policy in favour of reliance on purely automatic instruments. The great advantage of automatic stabilizers, it is claimed, is that no time is needed to ascertain the actual position of the economy or to obtain legislative sanction. All that is required is the time needed for actual changes to take effect. Provided that the automatic stabilizers work through instruments with reasonably immediate effects, e.g. progressive income taxation deducted at source or unemployment benefits, destabilizing movements will not be induced in consequence. Thus, it is argued, the objective should be to dispense with discretionary measures and attempt to improve the automatic stabilizers already included within the monetary-fiscal framework.

Whilst persuasively argued, the case for reliance solely upon automatic stabilizers is difficult to defend. On the one hand, as we have previously pointed out in the introductory chapters of this volume, automatic stabilizers cut both ways. They may weaken the force of destabilizing movements within the economy, but they also weaken the stabilizing forces towards recovery when income levels depart from their desired values. On the other hand, it is extremely difficult to design automatic fiscal stabilizers which exert both significant and non-perverse impacts in all situations. In principle, in simple linear national income models, automatic stabilizing devices incorporating the principle of formula flexibility[2] may contain income fluctuations within very narrow limits; in practice, when allowance is made for all the potential response patterns of the private sector, including asymmetrical responses between the upswings and downswings of the trade cycle, it becomes extremely difficult to guarantee that such devices may not, on occasion, produce perverse destabilizing results.

For this reason, attempts to incorporate automatic stabilizers within the fiscal system have usually relied upon the concept of built-in flexibility of the tax system[3] The degree of built-in flexibility of the tax system is measured by the responsiveness of tax receipts to income change, dT/dy_1. If $dT/dY > 0$, then the system exhibits built-in flexibility. Generally, the greater the degree of built-in flexibility, the greater the degree of automatic stabilization incorporated within the fiscal system, although it has long been realized that built-in flexibility cannot fully offset a destabilizing income change arising from some autonomous disturbance.[4] Moreover, recent theoretical work has highlighted the conceptual distinction between built-in flexibility and automatic stabilization. One argument has shown that automatic stabilizers may overshoot their mark when integrated into a simple growth model with progressive taxation.[5] Another argues that a suitably lagged consumption function combined with multiplier-accelerator analysis can result in greater instability for the economy with built-in flexibility than without.[6] Having indicated the essential points of what is admittedly a difficult branch of fiscal policy, we turn now to a more formal analysis.

III. A SHORT-TERM DYNAMIC MODEL

Let us adopt a simple national income model which combines the accelerator principle with the Keynesian multiplier.[7] With a closed economy, national income at time n is given by

$$Y_n \equiv C_n + I_n + G_n$$

Consumption we assume to be a linear function of income in the previous period and we simplify the analysis by assuming average and marginal propensities to be equal; i.e. we dispense with consumption at zero income. Accordingly we have

$$C_n = bY_{n-1}$$

Investment we assume to be geared to changes in consumer demand. A simple version of the accelerator concept makes investment depend upon the change in consumption over the previous period. Thus we may write

$$I_n = \Omega(C_n - C_{n-1})$$

or alternatively

$$I_n = b\Omega Y_{n-1} - b\Omega Y_{n-2}$$

Finally, we assume that at some stage in the past the government launched an expenditure programme, e.g. for defence, and has maintained its defensive commitment at a constant level ever since.

Thus

$$G_n = G_{n-1} = G_{n-2} = \ldots G_{n-n} = \overline{G}$$

The level of national income is now given by

$$Y_n = b(1 + \Omega)Y_{n-1} - b\Omega Y_{n-2} + \overline{G} \qquad (VI.1)$$

That is to say, the level of national income for any period is uniquely determined by a non-homogeneous second-order difference equation with constant coefficients. Its solution is a comparatively straightforward exercise given by the equation

$$Y_n = k_1 x_1^n + k_2 x_2^n + \frac{-d}{a+b+c} \qquad (VI.2)$$

where $a = 1$
$b = -b(1 + \Omega)$
$c = b\Omega$
$d = -G$

and where x_1 and x_2 are the solution to the quadratic equation, $ax^2 + bx + c = 0$, obtained in the usual way, [8] and where k_1 and k_2 are found by comparing two given initial conditions or income levels. [9] The equation is non-homogeneous owing to the constant level of government expenditures. In the absence of taxation, this constancy of government spending implies that we are dealing with a model of income determination which has no discretionary stabilizing element. These assumptions are sufficient to generate a time sequence of income change whose character is determined solely by the values we assign to the multiplier and accelerator coefficients. There are four possible cases to consider. At one extreme a zero or low value of the accelerator may be sufficiently dwarfed by the multiplier so that the initial expenditure by the government sector leads to a raising of the income level to a new equilibrium which is then maintained as a constant. This is in accordance with the simple Keynesian case where investment is assumed exogenous. At the opposite extreme, a high value of the accelerator is sufficient to generate an explosive movement of income which rises without limit. (10) For our purpose it is the intermediate cases which are of greater interest. Depending upon the values we select for the multiplier and the accelerator we may generate a continual cyclical movement of income which displays either damped or increasingly unstable fluctuations. These cases are illustrated in Figure VI.2 together with the intermediate borderline case where the opposing influences are just exactly offset culminating in a cyclical movement of constant magnitude.

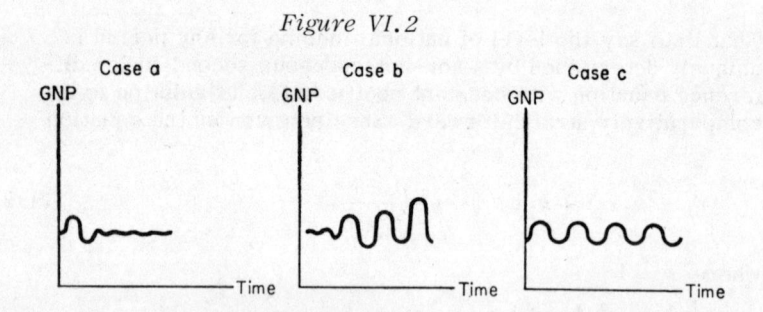

Figure VI.2

The foregoing has assumed the absence of discretionary stabilization policy. Let us now modify the analysis by assuming that the government expenditure programme is designed to act in a counter-cyclical manner. Our purpose is to show that discretionary changes by the government sector may heighten the degree of instability already inherent within the system.

Again let us assume that the government maintains its defence expenditure at a constant level, irrespective of the income level.

In addition, however, we now assume that, following the initial period in which the defence programme was established, additional outlays are incurred or cut back in the attempt to stabilize the economy. Suppose that the government is aiming at a 'target' level of income Y^* compatible with full employment. If income in the previous period falls short of the target level, additional outlays are incurred in the current period; if income in the previous period exceeds the target level, expenditures are reduced. Thus we assume that the government reacts to income changes with a one-period lag just as consumers do, but in the opposite direction. In this case our government expenditures function may be written

$$G_n = G_d + \mu(Y_{n-1} - Y^*)$$

where G_d represents the constant defence expenditure and μ is the stabilization coefficient. μ is of course negative; we may also assume that μ is less than unity. The government, having mastered the intricacies of multiplier analysis in the initial part of this volume, will adjust μ to its estimate of the marginal propensity to save. It will not attempt to make up any shortfall in the desired level of income entirely by itself. Such a policy would clearly overshoot the mark and be destabilizing but this is obviously a trivial case. Rather, μ will be increased when b falls and vice versa. Thus our assumptions postulate no more than what appears to be rational sophisticated behaviour upon the part of the government desirous of stabilizing the income level at Y^*. What are the consequences?

To answer this question let us refer to the rather special Case c illustrated in Figure VI.2. Here it is assumed that the values of the multiplier and accelerator coefficients are just sufficient—with government expenditures held constant—to generate continuous regular fluctuations in income which neither die out nor become explosive, but are maintained at a given magnitude. Superimposed upon this model, the modified expenditures equation is sufficient to generate increased cyclical instability without necessarily changing the character of the income sequence. The cycles continue indefinitely as before but are now of a more violent and unstable nature as a consequence of compensatory expenditure changes.

A numerical example may serve to clarify the argument. Let us assume that the marginal propensity to consume is equal to 0·5, implying a multiplier of 2, and the accelerator coefficient is 2.

If defence expenditures are maintained at a level of 1 (billion) then, in the absence of compensatory expenditures changes, the income sequence will be as shown in section A of Table VI.1. This example is one provided by Samuelson in his initial article.[11] Consider now the compensatory expenditures func-

Table VI.1

	A		B	
$Y_n = b(1+\Omega)Y_{n-1} - b\Omega Y_{n-2} + 1$			$Y_n = b(1+\Omega)Y_{n-1} - b\Omega Y_{n-2}$ $+ 1 + \mu(Y_{n-1} - Y^*)$	
$b = 0\cdot 5; \Omega = 2$			$b = 0\cdot 5; \Omega = 2; \mu = -0\cdot 5; Y^* = 3$	
Period	Y_n	G_n	Y_n	G_n
1	1·0	1·0	1·0	1·0
2	2·5	1·0	3·5	2·0
3	3·75	1·0	5·0	0·75
4	4·125	1·0	4·0	0·00
5	3·4375	1·0	1·5	0·50
6	2·0313	1·0	0·0	1·75
7	0·6094	1·0	1·0	2·50
8	−0·1172	1·0	3·5	2·00
9	0·2148	1·0	5·0	0·75
10	1·4395	1·0	4·0	0·0
11	2·9443	1·0	1·5	0·5
12	3·9771	1·0	0·0	1·75
13	4·0212	1·0	1·0	2·50
14	3·0548	1·0	3·5	2·0
15	1·5610	1·0	5·0	0·75
16	0·2867	1·0	4·0	0·0
17	−0·1310	1·0	1·5	0·5
18	0·5169	1·0	0·0	1·75
19	1·9063	1·0	1·0	2·50
20	3·3427	1·0	3·5	2·00
21	4·1076	1·0	5·0	0·75
22	3·8188	1·0	4·0	0·0
.	.	.	.	.
.	.	.	.	.
.	.	.	.	.

tion with the stabilization coefficient −0·5. This implies that the government, taking the size of the multiplier into account, attempts to rectify any divergence from the target level of income by an expenditure change of 50 per cent of the discrepancy in the reverse direction. We also assume that the target income level is 3 (billion). The results are summarized in section B of Table VI.1.

Thus not only does the adoption of countercyclical expenditures policy increase the magnitude of fluctuation between peak and trough, but the cyclical movement itself is speeded up. Compensatory policy serves to increase the frequency of the trade cycle. The comparative positions are summarized in Figure VI.3.

Figure VI.3 Fluctuations in Y_n with and without compensatory expenditures

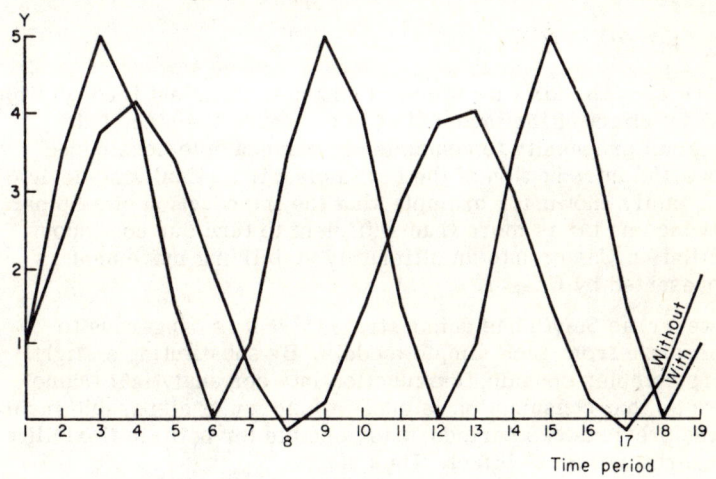

It remains to enquire into the cause of this destabilizing impact. The answer is comparatively simple and can be given without delving into the mathematics of difference equations. It stems from the fact that by adopting a target level of income the government is behaving in what is an essentially arbitrary and random manner. If income in the period $n - 1$ exceeds the target level, the government cuts back upon its planned level of expenditures *irrespective* of the response of investment in the private sector. Clearly, as long as the investment sector is concerned solely with the change in the volume of consumer demand, this decrease in government spending may coincide with expansionary or contractionary movements as the case may be. Our policy measure may be compared to the percussion player who strikes the timpani every time the conductor looks in his direction. On occasions it may help the performance along; more often it will not.

IV. AUTOMATIC STABILIZATION IN A DYNAMIC SETTING

(a) The short-term case

If the case against countercyclical policy is that it may intensify cyclical movements, what is the case for automatic stabilization? It is a simple matter to take account of built-in flexibility merely by adopting a proportional income tax. In this case our consumption function becomes

$$C_n = b(1 - t_y)Y_{n-1}$$

where t_y is the tax rate which is assumed invariant through time. The net effect of the income tax is to reduce the size of the marginal propensity to consume. In our example considered above, the introduction of the tax is clearly a stabilizing device; it is easily shown, for example, that the introduction of a 50 per cent income tax is more than sufficient to turn our continuous oscillation Case c into an ultimately stabilizing movement as represented by Case a.

However, as Smyth has demonstrated [12] it is dangerous to generalize from such simple models. By substituting a slightly more complex consumption function into our analytical framework so that consumption is made a function of disposable income of the previous two periods, it is possible for built-in flexibility to exert a perverse effect. Thus, if

$$C_n = b_1(1 - t_y)Y_{n-1} + b_2(1 - t_y)Y_{n-2}$$

where

$$0 < b_1 < 1, 0 < b_2 < 1, 0 < b_1 + b_2 < 1$$

then under certain conditions [13] the presence of built-in flexibility, as indicated by the proportional income tax, will increase the extent of instability. Moreover, in certain cases, it is possible for the existence of built-in flexibility to turn a damped oscillatory movement of income, as in Case *a* of Figure VI. 2, into an increasingly unstable situation, as indicated in Case *b*.

(b) *The long-run case*

Thus far, we have dealt with the question of built-in flexibility, and the resultant degree of automatic stabilization in a short-term setting. In this case, built-in flexibility is assumed to exist when tax receipts vary directly and positively with income changes. In contrast, built-in flexibility would be absent in the case where tax revenues were autonomously determined and independent of the income level. When we turn to a simple-growth model, however, the question must be raised as to whether or not such a definition is appropriate. If, in a growing economy, income is expanding constantly over time we would naturally expect a similar expansion of fiscal revenue without considering this in any way to be an indication of built-in flexibility. [14] For positive built-in flexibility to exist within a growth context, we shall require that the fiscal system behaves in a progressive fashion, i.e. that the tax revenue grows more than proportionately to income. Conversely, we shall assume that the absence of built-in flexibility is indicated by fiscal receipts' remaining a constant proportion of national income.

Having defined built-in flexibility of the fiscal system in this manner, a modified Harrod-Domar model is sufficient to demonstrate our basic point, namely that in an expanding economy the presence of built-in flexibility may be too potent and may cause the system to overshoot the equilibrium growth path of income. The model presented here differs slightly from the formulation adopted in Chapter V [15]. There it was sufficient to demonstrate that taxes and government expenditures could influence the long-term growth path of income necessary for full employment of the capital stock. For that purpose a simple Domar formulation with autonomous investment spending was quite sufficient; there was no need to involve ourselves with the intricacies of difference equations. Now, however, a more complex policy problem requires more complex tools of analysis; again we will invoke second-order difference equations. [16]

Following our analysis of Chapter V, let us again assume that the increase in capacity income in any period, n, is a simple function of investment in the previous period, irrespective of whether the investment is undertaken by the private or the public sector.

Thus again we may write

$$\Delta Y_n^c = h(I_{n-1} + pG_{n-1})$$

where h is again the output-capital ratio and p is that percentage of government expenditure assumed to be of a capacity-creating character. Let us also assume, however, that investment by the private sector is itself a function of the income level of the same period. Thus

$$I_n = \Omega Y_n$$

where Ω is an accelerator coefficient for the private sector. Let us further assume that the proportion of government expenditure upon investment activities, p, remains a constant, and that total government expenditure is also a constant function of the level of national income. In this case, we may write

$$G_n = gY_n \text{ and } pG_n = pgY_n$$

It follows that the total of resources channelled into investment activities, whether by the private or the public sector, in any period, n, is simply

$$\Omega Y_n + pgY_n = \rho_n$$

where ρ is a constant proportion of national income. Accordingly, the increase in capacity income is simply given by

$$\Delta Y_n^c = h\rho$$

On the demand side of the economy, national income in money terms is given, as before, by the conventional identity

$$Y_n^m \equiv C_n^m + I_n^m + G_n^m$$

Now, however, let us assume that consumption is a lagged function of disposable income of the previous period. In this case we have

$$C_n^m = bY_{n-1}^m(1 - t_y)$$

where t_y is the average rate of tax and is assumed to be constant; i.e. there is no built-in flexibility in the sense defined above. Investment by the private sector we know to be a constant function of income in the same period, and likewise government expenditure is also given as a constant proportion of national income. Thus,

$$I_n^m = \Omega Y_n^m$$

$$G_n^m = g Y_n^m$$

The level of money national income at period n therefore is obtained simply by solving the linear difference equation so that

$$Y_n^m = \left[\frac{b(1-t)}{1-(\Omega+g)}\right]^n Y_0^m$$

which may be written

$$\frac{\Delta Y^m}{Y} = \frac{b(1-t)}{1-(\Omega+g)} - 1$$

Equilibrium growth thus requires the increase in monetary national income to equal the increase in capacity output so that

$$\frac{b(1-t)}{1-(\Omega+g)} = h\rho + 1$$

The numerical example in Table VI.2 illustrates the equilibrium growth path, assuming arbitrary values of the coefficients.

The example illustrates the case where the economy moves along the equilibrium path, growth requirements being fulfilled without inflation. Following established convention, we associate changes in the price index with the divergence of the paths of equilibrium growth and actual growth of national income, so that the price index is given by the following formula:

$$P = \frac{1+(\Delta Y^m/Y^m)}{1+(\Delta Y^r/Y^r)} \cdot 100$$

In our 'equilibrium' example the price index displays no movement in view of this convention.

Table VI.2 *Equilibrium Growth*

$$(b = \cdot 9; t = \cdot 1; g = \cdot 1; \rho = \cdot 15; h = \cdot 53)$$

Periods	Y^r	Y^m	C^m	G^m	T^m	S^m Govt. ($T^m - G^m$)	S^m Private ($Y^m - C^m + T^m$)	I^m	Price index
1	1000	=1000	750	100	100	—	150	150	100
2	1080	=1080	810	108	108	—	162	162	100
3	1166	=1166	875	117	117	—	174	174	100
4	1259	=1259	944	126	126	—	189	189	100
.	.	.	.	.	.	.	.	.	.
.	.	.	.	.	.	.	.	.	.
.	.	.	.	.	.	.	.	.	.

Clearly, if there is an upward change in the coefficients b or g, i.e. a rise in the rate of consumer or government expenditure, then, with no change in the tax coefficient, the actual growth of money income will exceed the equilibrium growth and the general price level will rise at an increasing rate. In the case of a rise in the investment coefficient, the general result does not differ, but the inflationary movement is partially offset by the effect of the real rise in the rate of investment on the equilibrium rate of growth. In other words, in a 'no flexibility' situation as defined for the growth case, an inflationary movement caused by an increase in one or more of the spending coefficients will not be offset by the rise in tax receipts.

We now consider the effects of two autonomous changes which have the same initial impact on the level of national income. We shall first of all assume an upward change in the investment coefficient, ρ, and secondly an upward change by the same amount in the government expenditure coefficient, g.

The only other change we allow is in the tax system. It is now assumed that a progressive rate structure obtains, so that a rise in income produces a more than proportionate rise in tax revenue and thus a rise in the average rate of tax. In short, the value of the tax coefficient depends on the rate of change of income which can be represented in the following formula:[17]

$$t_{yn} = t_{yn-1} + \mu(Y_{n-1} - Y_{n-2})$$

(c) *Change in the investment coefficient, ρ*

Using the above equations and assuming a rise in ρ, the system will be disequilibrated. The rise in investment will increase the rate of income generation, producing an initial inflationary effect. However, this effect will be gradually offset by two forces. The first is the effect of the rise in the rate of net investment on the real rate of growth. The second is the rise in the value of the tax coefficient, t_y, caused by the process of income generation itself. At some point in time, the path of growth tendencies will cross the path of the equilibrium growth of income. This must be so because, with all coefficients constant with the exception of t_y, which rises as national income rises, money national income will grow, but at a decreasing rate, while the equilibrium rate of increase will remain constant; i.e. equilibrium national income will rise exponentially. At some point, therefore, the built-in flexibility of the tax system will make the system 'overshoot' the mark as the path of actual income generation crosses the equilibrium growth path. This situation contrasts with that found in the macro-static case, where with a progressive tax system it is not even possible to re-establish the full employment level of national income at a predetermined price level. The point at which the paths of actual income and equilibrium income will cross will depend on the extent of the change in ρ, the value of μ and the lag in tax assessment.

A second numerical example (Table VI.3) will perhaps clarify these results, which spring essentially from the fact that, with a progressive tax structure, the process of growth generates increases in fiscal receipts in excess of the growth of public expenditures. The induced deflationary impact increases with the passage of time; ultimately it becomes sufficient to 'over-stabilize' the economy and force a level of national income below the equilibrium level.

This phenomenon, that of a continuous raising of the fiscal surplus, has received wide attention in recent years, especially in the United States where it has been termed the 'fiscal drag' and linked with another important concept, that of the full employment budget surplus. The latter may be defined simply as the potential budget surplus which would obtain at a full employment level of income, given existing expenditure patterns and tax rates. Diagrammatically, we can convey the essence of the argument in Figure VI.4. Here it is assumed that the fiscal surplus is a

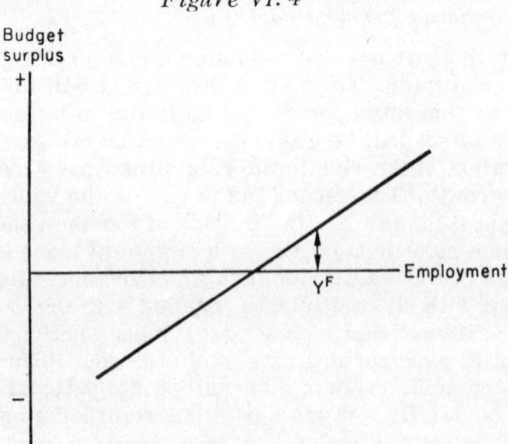

Figure VI.4

Table VI.3. *Built-in Flexibility and Growth; Case I*
($b = \cdot 9; t_1 = \cdot 1; \mu = \cdot 0003; g = \cdot 1; \rho = \cdot 2; h = \cdot 53$)

Period	Y^r	Y^m	C^m	G^m	T^m	S^m Govt.	S^m Private	I^m	P
1	1000	=1000	750	100	100	—	150	150	100
2	1080	<1157	810	116	116	—	231	231	107
3	1194	<1269	888	127	187	60	194	254	106·3
4	1321	<1336	936	134	241	107	161	267	101·1
5	1461	>1373	961	137	275	138	137	275	93·9
.	.	.	.	.	.	.	.	.	.
.	.	.	.	.	.	.	.	.	.
.	.	.	.	.	.	.	.	.	.

direct function of employment level, assuming expenditure policies and tax rates remain unchanged. At full employment a small budget surplus is attained. At less than full employment the surplus is speedily eliminated and a deficit results as expenditure is increased (unemployment benefits, welfare payments, etc.) and as tax revenues fall. Conversely, as the income level exceeds the full employment level, implying inflationary conditions, a larger fiscal surplus is automatically generated due to both the normal expansion of fiscal receipts and the cutback in government relief and assistance payments. The slope of the function, therefore, indicates the degree of built-in flexibility of the budget system.[18]

Whereas the slope of the function provides a measure of the built-in flexibility of the budget, a parametric shift of the function would imply a discretionary fiscal change, on either the tax side, the expenditure side or both. So far, our discussion of the full-employment budget surplus has been static in nature in that we have taken a snapshot of the function at a given point in time. Now, however, let us allow for dynamic changes. If, as we have indicated, economic expansion is accompanied by an expansion of fiscal receipts in excess of increased expenditure, then over time the fiscal surplus will be increased for any given employment level.[19] The budget function will shift gradually upwards as revenue expansion outpaces expenditure growth. This is the nature of the 'fiscal drag' which is thus tantamount to a discretionary restrictionary fiscal change. The concern was voiced in the late 1950s and early 1960s that this continued tendency would exert a progressively deflationary impact upon the economy and slow the rate of economic growth. If the nature of fiscal drag is akin to restrictive discretionary measures then is not the remedy immediately apparent, namely that of a phased decrease in the rate of tax over time?

But this is precisely the solution to our problem of over-stabilization of the fiscal system when tax rates are progressive. The problem of fiscal drag and that of excessive automatic stabilization are essentially one and the same; they both spring from the desire of modern societies to incorporate a degree of progressivity within the fiscal system. As long as this remains the case, the solution must lie in the ability and willingness to adopt discretionary policies, to offset the undesirable consequence of combining progressivity and economic growth.[20]

To argue that automatic stabilizers are inadequate, or involve undesirable consequences necessitating compensatory action, does not resolve entirely the choice between discretionary fiscal changes and reliance upon automatic weapons. The question of degree remains; to what extent should discretionary changes be invoked? Even if automatic stabilizers cannot be ever fully adequate should we still not try to make the system as automatically stabilizing as possible? Unfortunately there appears to be no simple answer to these questions. On the one hand, a value judgement is involved as to how far should discretionary action be permitted to interfere with the normal functioning of the market economy. On the other, the political feasibility of enacting discretionary fiscal changes may be vital in determining the outcome. In the United Kingdom the comparative ease and speed of obtaining legislative approval would tend to support the case for discretionary changes. In contrast, in the United States the comparative difficulty of obtaining legislative sanction, and the great uncertainty surrounding the timing of policy changes, would tend to reinforce the arguments for reliance upon automatic stabilizers and perhaps also for greater dependence upon monetary policy.[21] For our purposes, it is sufficient to note that logical difficulties confront either policy, and when considered in a dynamic setting such difficulties are generally enhanced.

NOTES

[1] Introducing finite time periods into the analysis, requiring the prior dating of quantity variables, is an insufficient condition for a truly dynamic treatment of fiscal policy. Indeed, the comparative static methodology may still be employed by focusing upon the adjustment process *at any given point in time*. Nonetheless, by allowing the analysis of disequilibrium states it takes an important first step towards a dynamic treatment. For various definitions of static versus dynamic analysis see especially William J. Baumol, *Economic Dynamics*, 3rd edn., Macmillan, London, 1970, Ch. 1.

[2] Formula flexibility refers to the situation where previously legislated tax or expenditure changes are called into effect by some predetermined index. An example might be the halving of social security payments when unemployment exceeded, say, one million workers.

[3] Transfer payments etc. can be incorporated into the analysis merely by being treated as negative taxes.

[4] R. A. Musgrave and M. H. Miller, 'Built-in Flexibility', *American Economic Review*, March 1948.

[5] A. T. Peacock, 'Built-in Flexibility and Economic Growth' in Gottfried Bombach (ed.), *Stabile Preise in Wachsender Wirtschaft*, Tübingen, 1960.

(6) D. J. Smyth, 'Can Automatic Stabilizers Be Destabilizing?', *Public Finance*, 1963. Smyth's article, it will be noted, really involves a misnomer. To the question 'Can automatic stabilizers be destabilizing?' the answer must be unmistakably no, by definition. A more accurate title—although lacking the same dramatic impact—would have been: 'Can built-in flexibility be destabilizing?' to which, as Smyth has demonstrated, an affirmative answer is possible.

(7) The model presented here follows Paul A. Samuelson's classic article, 'Interactions between the Multiplier Analysis and the Principle of Acceleration', *Review of Economic Statistics*, May 1939.

(8) I.e. by $x = \dfrac{-b \pm \sqrt{(b^2 - 4ac)}}{2a}$

(9) A useful introduction to the solution of difference equations which deals specifically with the Samuelson model is given by W. J. Baumol, op. cit., pp. 151 ff.

(10) It is this case which forms the basis of the Hicksian theory of the trade cycle. Cf. J. R. Hicks, *A Contribution to the Theory of the Trade Cycle*, Oxford University Press, London, 1950.

(11) In the original article the income level for period seven is incorrectly given as 0·9141.

(12) D. J. Smyth, op. cit.

(13) I.e. if the roots of the characteristic equation are complex.

(14) To consider an extreme example, in a growing economy even a window tax would generate additional revenues over time; one would hesitate to cite this as an example of built-in flexibility of the fiscal system, however.

(15) The model presented here is in fact taken from A. T. Peacock, op. cit.

(16) To which, we were assured, there is no general solution, the equations being non-linear. For this reason we will again utilize numerical examples.

(17) It must be admitted straight away that a two-period lag in adjustment of the rate structure is adopted for analytical convenience. It is quite realistic to assume that tax liabilities are not lagged while tax assessments and payments are, but it is a moot point whether taxpayers' consumption is a function of income after actual tax deducted or after allowing for tax liabilities, i.e. whether taxpayers think in 'cash' or 'accrual' terms. It is assumed here that they think in cash terms—like the authors.

(18) It is important to note, however, that it does not in any way indicate the degree of automatic stabilization incorporated into the budget system. This is because the multiplier impact of an expenditure change will—according to the balanced budget theorem—normally differ from that of a tax change. Consequently, it is quite possible for a

decrease in the extent of the fiscal surplus to exert a deflationary impact upon the overall economy, if it is attained by the combined workings of a tax and expenditure decrease where the fall in revenues exceeds the decline in expenditures. The concept of the full employment budget surplus, therefore, should be used with caution when considered as an index of the degree of automatic stabilization.

(19) The full employment level being, of course, defined in percentage terms.

(20) Although this conclusion may be questioned; see in particular, Vito Tanzi, 'A Proposal for a Dynamically Self-Adjusting Personal Income Tax', *Public Finance,* No. 4, 1966, for an interesting alternative solution. What Tanzi's approach really amounts to is a variant of formula flexibility which fundamentally is no different in principle from reliance on built-in flexibility.

(21) Not requiring the approval of Congress.

Appendix to Part I

A SIMPLE NON-LINEAR MODEL OF FISCAL POLICY

I. INTRODUCTION

Most of our models have been constructed with linear functions. One could argue that the parameters in the equations would, in practice, be capable of estimation, and that there is no need to assume that throughout the time period in which the values of aggregates are being observed the values of the parameters need remain constant. However, once it is agreed that non-linear functions would better represent our hypotheses about firms' and households' behaviour, it becomes rather tedious to keep changing the values of the fixed parameters throughout the process of adjustment from one initial equilibrium position to another. Building on previous elementary mathematical techniques, it is a relatively simple matter to generalize the models used and, in particular, to remove the restriction of linearity.

Another characteristic of our models is that the specification of the parameters in the equations results in a proliferation of symbols. Once it is recognized that a particular variable depends on more than one independent variable, e.g. consumption being a function of both income and the rate of interest, very complicated expressions emerge, a good example being equation II.6. A generalized model which concentrates on functional relationships rather than the exact nature of the underlying equations, e.g. $i = i(Y, MS)$ rather than $i = (vY + \gamma - MS)/c$, gets round this difficulty. Alternatively, for roughly the same 'input' of symbols, we can examine more complicated and possibly more realistic hypotheses.

In what follows, we shall build a non-linear system which includes some of the main features of previous models. The mathematical techniques used are total differentiation and matrix multiplication, which have already been employed separately in previous analysis.

II. A SIMPLE NON-LINEAR MODEL

We shall first of all employ a simple model, very similar to the one used in Chapter IV, for an open economy, with a government sector and which includes a monetary equation as well as income equation.

$$Y = C + I + G + X - M$$
$$C = C[Y(1 - t_y) - \eta]$$
$$I = I(i)$$
$$M = M(Y)$$
$$i = i(Y, MS)$$

where G, X and MS are autonomous variables and defined as before

$M =$ imports
$C =$ private consumption
$t_y =$ proportional income tax rate
$\eta =$ taxes invariant with income, and is also autonomous
$i =$ bond rate of interest.

It will be noted that the various expressions above are put in functional form. The exact nature of the equations is not specified. For example, $I = I(i)$ means that investment is a function of the rate of interest, but we do not specify the exact nature of the function as we did previously in making it a linear function of the rate of interest.

On examination, we find that we can reduce these functional relationships to three equations with three unknowns, I, M and i, and with three fiscal policy variables, G, T and t_y. Thus

$$Y = C[Y(1 - t_y) - \bar{\eta}] + I(i) + \overline{G} + \overline{X} - \overline{M}$$
$$M = M(Y)$$
$$i = i(Y, \overline{MS})$$

Taking the total derivatives of each equation and rearranging terms, we obtain the following:

$$\left. \begin{array}{l} dY[1 - (1 - t_y)C_y] + dM - I_i di = dG + dX - C_y d\eta \\ -M_y dY + dM = 0 \\ -i_y dY + di = i_{MS} dMS \end{array} \right\} \quad \text{(A.1)}$$

which may be written as

$$\begin{bmatrix} C^X & 1 & -I_i \\ -M_y & 1 & 0 \\ -i_y & 0 & 1 \end{bmatrix} \begin{bmatrix} dY \\ dM \\ di \end{bmatrix} = \begin{bmatrix} dG + dX - C_y d\eta \\ 0 \\ i_{MS} dMS \end{bmatrix} \quad (A.2)$$

where $C^X = 1 - (1-t)C_y$. The subscripts denote partial derivatives, so that, for example,

$$M_y dY = \frac{\partial M}{\partial y} \cdot dY$$

Inverting the matrix we obtain

$$\begin{bmatrix} dY \\ dM \\ di \end{bmatrix} = \frac{1}{\Delta} \begin{bmatrix} 1 & -1 & I_i \\ M_y & C^X - I_i i_y & I_i M_y \\ i_y & -i_y & C^X + M_y \end{bmatrix} \begin{bmatrix} dG + dX - Cd\eta \\ 0 \\ i_{MS} dMS \end{bmatrix} \quad (A.3)$$

where $\Delta = \det. A = C^X + M_y - i_y I i$.

In explaining the working of the model, we shall confine attention to the *direction of change* (+ or −) in the dependent variables (Y, M and i) resulting from a change in the value of the independent policy variables (G, T and M).

First of all, we determine the signs of the partial derivatives as follows:

$$0 < C_y, M_y, < 1; I_i, i_{MS} < 0; i_y > 0$$

In addition, $0 < t_y < 1$.

With this information, we find, first of all, that $\det. A = \Delta$ is positive. Further, we can now rewrite adj. A, substituting the signs for the partial derivatives. For example, if we take the element a_{32}, this is $+I_i(M_y)$. $I_i < 0$ and $M_y > 0$ so that the whole term is negative $[(+)(-)(+)]$.

$$\begin{bmatrix} dY \\ dM \\ di \end{bmatrix} = \frac{1}{\Delta} \begin{bmatrix} + & - & - \\ + & + & - \\ + & - & + \end{bmatrix} \begin{bmatrix} dG + dX - C_y d\eta \\ 0 \\ i_{MS} dMS \end{bmatrix}$$

Multiplying through in the usual manner, and listing our policy variables vertically and dependent variables horizontally, we can observe how the former change the value of the latter. We can add to our list of dependent variables the balance of payments change defined as $dB = dX - dM$. The direction of change will simply be determined by dM, with $dX = 0$. Similarly we can add to our list of independent variables the balanced budget change $dG + d\eta$ where $dG = d\eta$:

	Dependent Variables →	dY	dM	di	dB
Independent Variables	dG	+	+	+	−
	$d\eta$	−	−	−	+
	dMS	+	+	−	−
	$dG + d\eta$	+	+	+	−

While the direction of change can be determined by the model, what can we say about the magnitude of change? With MS exogenously determined, the model does not specify the nature of the monetary effects of any budgetary change. Consequently, if we change G, for example, any consequential effects on monetary supply which would affect the rate of interest, and, in turn, investment and income, are not recorded in the model. Nevertheless, we can reach the familiar conclusions about the effects of *equal* changes in G and η and also in the balanced budget. This is because, for example, if we compare an increase in G with an equal decrease in η and assume that the resultant initial deficit is financed by increases in cash, the expansion in money supply will be identical. Similarly, in the balanced budget case the initial change in the deficit/surplus is zero. There is therefore no reinforcing effect offered by changes in money supply.

Therefore, using expression A.3,

$$\frac{dY}{dG} = \frac{1}{\Delta}, \frac{dY}{d\eta} = -C_y \cdot \frac{1}{\Delta}, \frac{dY}{(dG + d\eta)} = (1 - C_y)\frac{1}{\Delta}$$

Clearly, pound for pound, an increase in government expenditure increases Y by a greater amount than a reduction in taxation of equal amount, the change in cash deficit being identical. Increasing G would have a greater multiplier effect than a balanced-budget change of equal amount, but an interesting curiosity is revealed by the fact that this result only follows for an equal decrease in η, if $C_y > 0\cdot5$!, given our model. This last comparison, however, stresses the need to consider monetary effects, for the tax change increases the supply of cash in the system, but the balanced budget does not.

III. FURTHER ANALYSIS

Having mastered the simple mathematical techniques displayed above and their application to fiscal policy models, the reader should try his hand at following some of the professional literature which has increasingly adopted the method of formulation explained in Section II above. Useful examples are:

D. J. and A. F. Ott, 'Monetary and Fiscal Policy: Goals and Choice of Instruments', *Quarterly Journal of Economics,* Vol. LXXXII, 1968;

R. N. Cooper, 'Macroeconomic Policy Adjustment in Interdependent Economies', *Quarterly Journal of Economics*, Vol. LXXXIII, 1969.

Both these articles also cover the subject matter of Chapter VII of this volume.

PART TWO

FISCAL POLICY AND THE THEORY
OF ECONOMIC POLICY

Chapter VII

POLICY TARGETS AND FISCAL INSTRUMENTS

I. INTRODUCTION

Thus far, our primary concern has been to outline the theory of fiscal policy, essentially in a Keynesian context, whilst focusing attention upon fluctuations in the aggregate level of output. On occasions we have utilized our output variable as a proxy for employment and prices; by extending the analysis to the external sector we have also dealt specifically with issues arising from balance of payments considerations. Throughout, however, in outlining the basic theory our conceptual framework has been essentially uni-dimensional. We have dealt with a single-valued objective function. Whilst changing the objective at will in order to extend the scope of our analysis we have nonetheless treated each objective in isolation. Although eminently suited to the process of model building it must be conceded that such a procedure drastically simplifies the problem of economic decision making when applied to the real world.

The first step in attaining greater realism in economic policy making is to recognize that both objectives and instruments are multi-dimensional. This entails specifying precisely both the goals to enter into the objective function and the policy tools available for their attainment. Two approaches are then possible. On the one hand we may assume that the policy objectives once specified are immutable; the question then reduces to combining sufficient policy instruments to realize their achievement. This we may refer to as the Hansen/Tinbergen approach to economic policy and it will be illustrated in the present chapter. A second approach we may refer to as the optimizing approach illustrated in the work of Theil. This discusses specifically the extent to which all or any of the policy goals may be modified in the event of conflict in order to maximize the welfare of society. The optimizing approach attempts to determine the extent to which all goals are to be compromised in order to maximize economic welfare given the preferences of society. In contrast, the Hansen/Tinbergen approach implies the search for new policy instruments by which all objectives may be achieved simultaneously. The following chapter will take up examples of the pragmatic approach of trade-off; for the present we will assume that policy objectives are immutable and we seek the policy tools for their attainment. The fundamental conclusion of the Hansen/Tinbergen analysis is that, given a specific number of policy targets, an equal number of policy instruments is required for their realization.

II. OBJECTIVE FUNCTION

For purposes of illustration let us assume that there are only two policy goals pertinent to the objective function, namely full employment and balance of payments equilibrium.[1]

Accordingly, our objective function may be expressed as

$$u = u(x, y)$$

where u represents the ordinal utility index which we are trying to maximize and x and y are the respective policy goals. We assume that there are values of x and y which will maximize the welfare of the decision maker. These values, which we assume correspond to full employment income and balance of payments equilibria, we denote by $\bar{x}$ and $\bar{y}$. Thus,

$$u(\bar{x}, \bar{y}) > \begin{matrix} u(\bar{x}, y) \\ u(x, y) \\ u(x, \bar{y}) \end{matrix}$$

Insisting upon the immutability of our policy objectives implies that no other values except $\bar{x}$ and $\bar{y}$ are admissible from the decision maker's standpoint. It follows that, as long as $\bar{x}$ and $\bar{y}$ are attained simultaneously, the choice of policy instruments is irrelevant. Any combination of instruments remains as good as any other providing the utility function is maximized.

III. THE MODEL

In all but the most trivial cases it is assumed that both objectives will respond to more than one policy instrument. This is the nature of interdependence which implies that no one policy tool may be uniquely related to any given target or objective. For present purposes let us assume that both objectives respond to fiscal policy—defined here to mean variations in the size of the budget surplus—as well as to monetary policy, denoted by changes in the level of interest rates. The essence of the argument may then be conveniently summarized in terms of Mundell's original diagram.

Figure VII.1

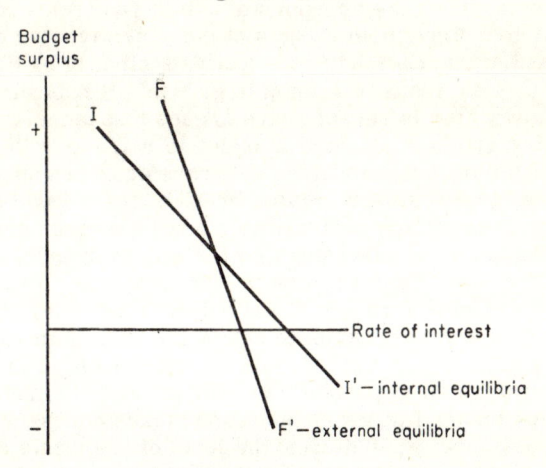

```
Budget
surplus
   |      F
  +|   I
   |
   |
   |_____ Rate of interest
   |        I'—internal equilibria
  -|        F'—external equilibria
```

In Figure VII.1 we measure the budget surplus, positive or negative, upon the vertical axis and the rate of interest upon the horizontal. Let us now consider all possible combinations of budget surplus and rate of interest consistent with the maintenance of full employment without inflation. Clearly, the locus of such a function will be negatively sloped since it is assumed that the deflationary impact of higher interest rates must be offset by an increase in spending if aggregate output is to be maintained. Similarly, consideration of all possible combinations consistent with balance of payments equilibria will reveal a negatively sloped function, since any decrease in the budget surplus will worsen the balance of trade,[2] and require a compensating improvement upon the capital account through higher interest rates. Let us now consider the slopes of the respective functions. The external function will possess the steeper slope. This follows from the fact that the balance of trade (exports minus imports) will be constant throughout the range of the employment function since both are a function of income. If capital is sensitive to interest rate movements, then a movement down the internal function implies a continual improvement upon the external account. In order to maintain equilibrium, therefore, a smaller interest-rate change will be needed to compensate any variation in the budget surplus in the case of the balance of payments function than in the case of the employment function. Thus the external function will possess the steeper slope and will intersect the internal function at a unique point which reconciles both internal and external policy requirements. Thus the appropriate use of two policy instruments enables us to achieve both targets of our objective function simultaneously. Let us now modify the analysis slightly by taking into consideration the issue of economic growth.[3] A popular policy proposal advocated in recent years argues that monetary and fiscal policy may be combined in order to raise growth rates. The essence of the proposal involves the transfer of resources from consumption to investment. Stated briefly, this is to be achieved by a strict fiscal policy designed to curtail existing consumption combined with an easy monetary policy and retirement of the debt aimed at inducing investment of the proceeds. Provided the correct mix of monetary and fiscal policy is pursued, virtually any rate of growth is considered attainable. The immediate appeal of such a policy lies in the fact that the attainment of successively higher growth rates is perfectly consistent with the maintenance of full employment, for, whilst increased taxes necessarily imply reduced consumer expenditures, the level of aggregate demand is maintained by the offsetting increase in investment activity. Accordingly, there need be no conflict between the goals of full employment and enhanced growth. The correct monetary-fiscal mix is designed to achieve both. Basically, the essence of the proposal may be reduced to one simple proposition: for any given level of budget surplus or deficit there will be but one specific rate of growth, provided the rate of interest is low enough to ensure investment of the available funds.

If we attempt to combine this analysis with the preceding argument, however, it follows at once that whatever combination of budget surplus and interest rate reconciles the internal and external equilibria conditions, this must also determine the growth rate. Once the equilibria conditions have been established, any attempt to raise the overall growth rate must be at the expense of internal or external stability—or indeed of both. And in view of the political impossibility of departing from the two stability conditions for any prolonged period of time, the growth rate ceases to be a policy variable; it becomes exogenously imposed upon the system. The pursuit of three interdependent objectives

Policy Targets and Fiscal Instruments 131

with only two policy instruments is logically impossible. One of the objectives must either be sacrificed or, as in the case of the growth rate, passively determined.

More formally, our objective function is now represented by the function

$$u = u(x, y, z)$$

where z is the growth objective. But as long as the permissible values for x and y are already determined so that $x = \bar{x}$ and $y = \bar{y}$, z is determined as a residual.

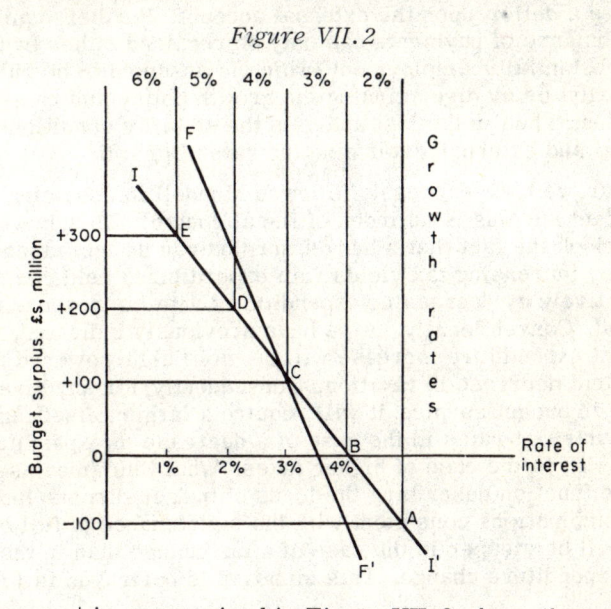

Figure VII.2

The argument is summarized in Figure VII. 2 where the rectangular areas denote the permissible growth rate applicable to any combination of interest rate and budget surplus. Thus a balanced budget is consistent with a 3 per cent growth rate, provided the rate of interest is 4 per cent. Equally, a £300 million budget surplus will allow a rate of growth of 6 per cent, assuming a rate of interest of 1 per cent. Let us assume an initial situation at point C. This satisfies both internal and external equilibrium conditions of the Mundellian model with a £100 million budget surplus and a 3 per cent interest rate. But such a combination also ensures a

4 per cent growth rate. Moreover, any attempt to increase the overall growth rate requires both higher taxes and lower interest rates. An additional £100 million in tax receipts together with a reduction of the interest rate to 2 per cent is needed to raise the growth rate by one percentage point—a movement from C to D. A raising of the growth rate is of course perfectly consistent with the maintenance of full employment. Indeed, since policy proposals for growth are designed to achieve both enhanced growth and full employment without inflation, the locus of points A to E, while tracing out what we may term the 'growth opportunity curve', is also coincident with the Mundellian internal stability function. It follows at once that adoption of a policy for a higher growth rate involves a deficit upon the external account. Further, equilibrium in the balance of payments can only be regained either by accepting substantial unemployment—which is assumed to be ruled out politically—or by discontinuing the growth policy and raising interest rates. Thus in the last analysis the stability conditions, both internal and external, determine the rate of growth.

Thus far, we have expressly followed Mundell in assuming that the budget surplus is an index of fiscal control. This, however, is to overlook the fact that a budget surplus can be increased in two ways: by increasing tax yields with expenditures held constant or alternatively by decreasing expenditures with tax revenues unchanged. Conventionally, as we have previously indicated, a government expenditure increase will be more high-powered than an equivalent decrease in taxation. Consequently, for any given increase in budget surplus, it will require a larger offsetting variation in interest rates in the case of a decrease in expenditures than it will in the case of higher taxes. What this amounts to is that the function describing the locus of budget surplus/interest rate combinations consistent with the maintenance of full employment will be steeper in the case of a tax change than in the case of an expenditure change. This situation is portrayed in Figure VII.3.

The diagram assumes an initial full employment equilibrium at point A, where the two functions coincide. Any movement along one of the functions implies a new equilibrium position where the functions will again intersect at a new combination of interest rate and budget surplus. Thus, if a combined tax increase and interest rate decrease leads to a new equilibrium at X, we immediately form a new internal function using G' as the expenditure function.

The introduction of the balanced budget multiplier principle modi-

Figure VII.3

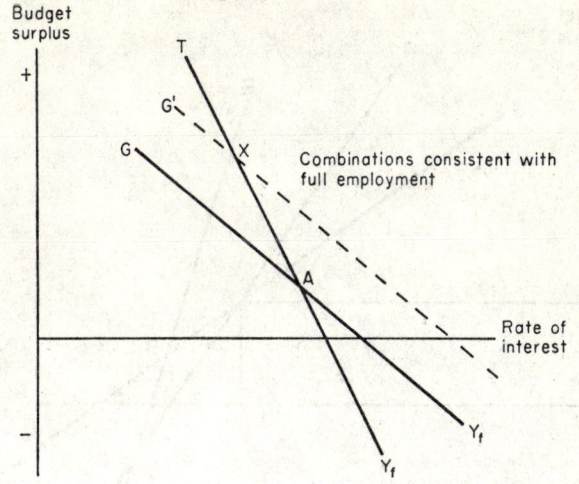

fies the pessimism of our original findings by permitting an element of choice over the permissible growth rate, for now there is more than one budget surplus/interest rate combination consistent with the maintenance of both internal and external equilibria. The analysis may be completed by reference to Figure VII.4.

In this case we assume an initial situation at position A. Although this is consistent with the maintenance of full employment it also implies a deficit upon the external account. Both full employment equilibria and balance of payments equilibria can be achieved either by increasing government expenditures and raising interest rates in moving to B or alternatively by decreasing taxes and raising interest rates as implied by position C (or, of course, by some combination of the two). From the growth viewpoint, position B will be preferred; the higher budget surplus and lower interest rate will be more conducive to investment.

The reader will appreciate that the discretionary power attained in the sphere of growth policy is a direct consequence of implicitly introducing another policy instrument—namely the size of the government sector for any given budget level. Economic growth becomes a policy variable because the number of instruments is brought into equality with the number of objectives.

The initial situation portrayed in Figure VII.4 assumes full employment income, combined with a balance of payments deficit.

Figure VII.4

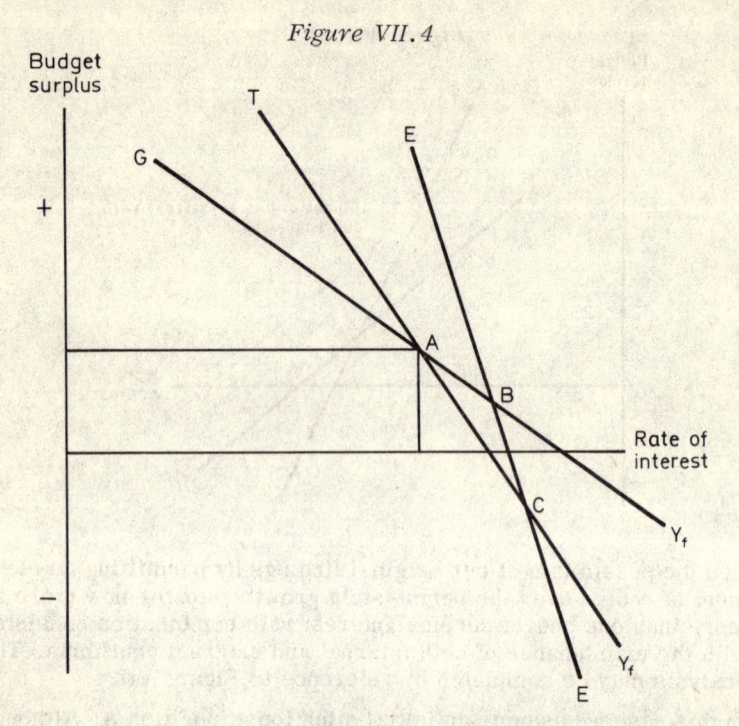

As we have seen, the optimal solution in terms of enhanced growth implies an increase in government spending as opposed to a decrease in taxation. Thus attainment of the optimal growth path would necessitate an increase in the ratio of public to private goods. This is most probably the situation in most countries with external deficits as, for example, the United Kingdom prior to the devaluation of 1967. There is, however, nothing inevitable in this outcome. Had the external function intersected the internal function to the left of point A, then the initial situation would have corresponded to full employment income and a payments surplus. Full equilibria would then have required an increased rate of taxation as opposed to a decrease in public spending, if the maximum permissible growth rate is to be attained. Since the tax proceeds are to be transferred to the private sector, no change would occur in the ratio of public to private goods. Thus one surprising conclusion of the analysis is that a payments deficit indicates the possible need to raise the public/private goods ratio, whilst a payments surplus has no such implication but merely suggests a change in the consumption/investment ratio in the private sector.

Whilst the additional policy instrument permits an area of discretion in determining the growth rate, it nonetheless remains true that an upper limit is imposed by the need to maintain both internal and external equilibria. Mathematically, we can express this as a simple problem in constrained maximization. In the present model the growth rate may be considered as a simple function of investment by the private sector plus government spending where the latter is of a capacity-creating character. Thus we may write

$$Y^g = \sigma(I + pG)$$

where Y^g symbolizes the growth rate of income and p is the proportion of government expenditures which are essentially in the nature of investment. The essence of the Mundellian analysis is that both employment and balance of payments equilibria may be considered a function of the budget surplus and interest rates. Thus

$$Y^F = Y^F(D, i)$$
$$B = B(D, i)$$

where D denotes the budget surplus and B the balance of payments surplus. Expressing the budget surplus in terms of expenditures and taxes—which permits us to take account of the modification introduced by the balanced budget multiplier—we have

$$Y^F = Y^F(G, T, i)$$
$$B = B(G, T, i)$$

where T is the tax yield. If full employment prevails initially it is still possible to vary G, T, and i whilst respecting the employment objective as long as the following condition is respected:

$$dY = \frac{\partial Y}{\partial G} \cdot dG + \frac{\partial Y}{\partial T} \cdot dT + \frac{\partial Y}{\partial i} \cdot di = 0$$

This we may refer to as the full employment constraint which traces out the boundaries of the internal stability function. Likewise, given initial balance of payments equilibria, variations in G, T, and i are permissible as long as the total differential is maintained at zero. Thus

$$dB = \frac{\partial B}{\partial G} \cdot dG + \frac{\partial B}{\partial T} \cdot dT + \frac{\partial B}{\partial i} \cdot di = 0$$

summarizes the balance of payments constraint, and traces out the external stability function. The permissible growth rate is then derived from the function:

$$\Pi = \sigma(I + \rho G) - \lambda_1 \left(\frac{\partial Y}{\partial G} \cdot dG + \frac{\partial Y}{\partial T} \cdot dT + \frac{\partial Y}{\partial i} \cdot di \right)$$

$$-\lambda_2 \left(\frac{\partial B}{\partial G} \cdot dG + \frac{\partial B}{\partial T} \cdot dT + \frac{\partial B}{\partial i} \cdot di \right)$$

where λ_1 and λ_2 are the undetermined Lagrange multipliers.

That the growth rate should be constrained arises from the fact that the third policy instrument is not a truly independent one. The size of the public sector is variable only within the limits of the budget surplus applicable to full employment income and balance of payments equilibria once the level of the budget has been determined. Given the inflexible nature of the full employment and balance of payments objectives, the permissible growth rate is again determined as a residual. Freeing the growth rate from this constraint would require a further policy tool, e.g. exchange rate flexibility, investment incentives, technological change and the like.

Nonetheless, the present analysis is useful in illustrating the nature of the maximization problem when one or more policy objectives is accorded priority. The constraint upon the permissible rate of growth disappears once employment levels and balance of payments surpluses are permitted to be variable. A social welfare function, possibly encompassing the preferences of generations yet unborn, might well allow a measure of unemployment in the interests of higher growth. This naturally leads us into the difficult question of trade-off, where no one objective is granted priority, *a priori*, over any other. This will be the subject matter of the following chapter.

NOTES

(1) Cf. the well-known article by R. A. Mundell, 'The Appropriate Use of Monetary and Fiscal Policy for Internal and External Stability', *IMF Staff Papers*, March 1962.

(2) Since any expansion of income leads to an increase of imports in excess of any induced expansion of exports. Cf. pp. 50-7.

(3) The following draws heavily upon a paper by one of the authors, G. K. Shaw: 'Monetary-Fiscal Policy for Growth and the Balance of Payments Constraint', *Economica*, May 1967.

Chapter VIII

FISCAL POLICY AND CONSTRAINED MAXIMIZATION

I. INTRODUCTION

As explained in Chapters I and VII, fiscal policy is not used in a policy situation in which it would be normal to have only one objective, represented by a single value of one macrovariable. In the policy situation facing governments, there may be several objectives to be met simultaneously, such as internal stability, balance of payments 'equilibrium', and a 'satisfactory' rate of economic growth. Nor is the budget the only instrument which may be used in order to attempt to meet the chosen objectives. Earlier chapters have indicated, at least implicitly, that an 'inactive' monetary policy may frustrate the operation of a fiscal policy in achieving only one objective represented by a 'target' value of national income.

In Chapter VII we saw that an important question is left unanswered if we think of the policy problem as one of achieving simultaneously two targets expressed in terms of single values of two macrovariables. If it is impossible to achieve both these values simultaneously, what is the 'best' policy to adopt? There is no particular reason why the 'next best' to not being able to achieve both values is to seek to achieve one, and to accept *any* value of the other which results from policy action. It may be that a preferred position would be one in which *neither* target value was achieved. Thus achieving a 'target' employment level in which 99 per cent of the working population were employed might mean, given the nature of the economy and the policy instruments available to influence its structure, accepting a rate of increase in the price level of 20 per cent per annum. At the other extreme, achieving complete price stability so that the rate of increase in the price level was zero might mean allowing the employment level to fall to, say, 92 per cent. There is good reason to suppose that, faced with these awkward facts of economic life, the community might prefer a lower employment level than the target value, if it meant a rate of increase in the price level lower than 20 per cent per annum. In contemporary jargon, it may be possible to identify the 'trade-off' between employment level and the rate of increase in price level which allows us to delineate a *preference function* for the community.

The analytical method which enables us to examine the problems posed by 'trade-off' between policy objectives may be introduced by considering the familiar example of the optimizing procedure of the individual household. We assume in microeconomic analysis that the household's objective is to maximize utility, subject to an income or expenditure constraint.

Expressed in the usual mathematical form, the utility of individual consumer, A, is a function of the commodities he buys; for simplicity we assume that there are only two commodities, l and m, which are competing substitutes, so that

$$u^A = u^A(l, m)$$

The consumer attempts to maximize this function subject to an income constraint. Assuming that all income is spent on l and m, and that the prices (P_1 and P_2) of l and m are given, then this constraint may be written

$$E(l, m) = P_1 l + P_2 m = Y^A$$

The algebraic solution to such an equation, which demonstrates how maximization of utility is achieved, need not be reproduced here, as it will be presented later in this chapter. Readers will be aware that its geometric counterpart is the tangency of the individual's highest indifference curve with the 'budget line' whose slope depends on the price ratio P_1/P_2. All that need be mentioned here is that it is possible to develop the analysis of constrained maximization situations in order to understand the role of fiscal policy in optimizing the welfare of the community, when welfare is no longer associated with only one variable, namely the level of national income.

It is clearly a big step from the specification of the individual utility function to some form of community indifference system, and from the simple 'budget line' registering the opportunities of the individual to purchase goods l and m to the identification of an analogous constraint on community choice. At the same time, as we hope to demonstrate, understanding the logic of constrained maximization is an important first step in the economist's comprehension of the problems of matching policy aims with the policy instruments which we have already examined.

II. EXAMPLE 1: THE EMPLOYMENT/INFLATION TRADE-OFF

In our first example, which is a highly simplified one, two policy objectives of the community are identified and are associated with two economic variables. The first is the price level, or rather its rate of change through time, i.e. $\dot{P} = (dP/dn)(1/P)$. The objective is to minimize the value of $\dot{P}$, subject, however, to achieving simultaneously a 'satisfactory' level of employment. The second objective, therefore, is to minimize the amount of unemployment, denoted by U. By definition, 'the best of all possible worlds' is reached when the values of both $\dot{P}$ and U are zero, which would be represented by the origin in a two-dimensional diagram with $\dot{P}$ measured along one axis and U along the other (see Figure VIII. 1). However, it is assumed that the 'cost' of reducing the value of $\dot{P}$ is a rise in the value of U. Following the conventions of welfare theory, we can draw a series of community indifference curves which delineate the 'trade-off' between the rate of price change and unemployment. We assume that over a specified range of $\dot{P}$ and U the indifference curves are both concave to the origin and also continuous. Thus, the 'trade-off' between $\dot{P}$ and U denotes that successive equal decrements of $\dot{P}$ can only be 'bought' by successive decrements of U of diminishing value. More formally, we describe the community's objective function, π, as

$$\pi = \pi(\dot{P}, U) \qquad (\text{VIII. 1})$$

where $\partial \pi / \partial \dot{P} < 0$ and $\partial \pi / \partial U < 0$.

Although it is not fundamental to the analysis, we may introduce two constraints. It would not be too unrealistic to assume that there is a maximum value of $\dot{P}$ which the community will tolerate, whatever the value of U, and, equally, a maximum value of U, whatever the value of $\dot{P}$; e.g. $\dot{P} = 10$ per cent per annum, and $U = 8$ per cent of the working population.

The community could reach its chosen nirvana at the origin, but this is not vouchsafed by the operation of the market economy. The 'opportunity slope' of the community is represented by the relationship between the rate of change in the price level and the unemployment rate which results from market forces. In this contribution, we shall conveniently domesticate for our use the Phillips curve, which is based on the relationship observed, in a number of countries, between the two variables. This relationship is represented by a downward sloping curve in a two-dimensional system with $\dot{P}$ on the vertical and U on the horizontal axis,

Figure VIII.1

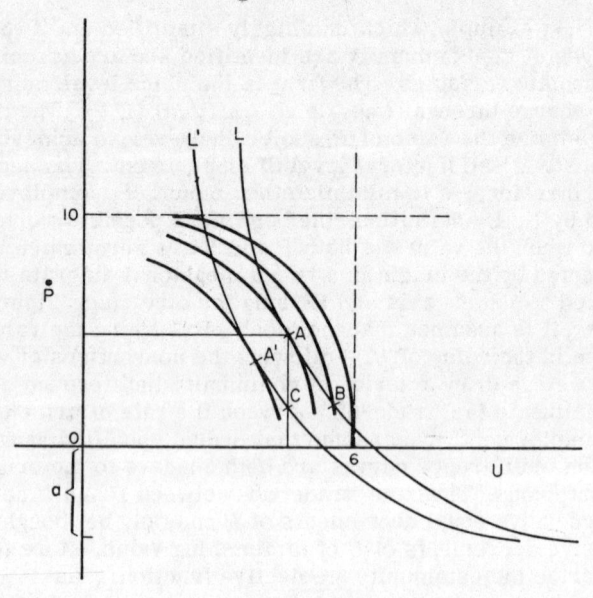

as shown by L in Figure VIII.1. For expositional purposes, we may assume that the relationship is dynamically stable over time, although it should be emphasized that recent explanations of rising unemployment and rising price levels have frequently invoked the spectre of a dynamically unstable Phillips curve which is being continually shifted outwards under the impact of adverse expectations surrounding future inflation rates. A common algebraic form of this relationship[1] is

$$\dot{P} = \epsilon + \zeta U^{-1} \qquad \text{(VIII.2)}$$

where $\epsilon < 0$ and $\zeta < 0$.

The problem of policy is to minimize $\dot{P}$ and U, subject to the constraint represented by the Phillips curve. The identification of the fulfilment of this condition is easy. It is simply the point of tangency between the Phillips curve and the highest (concave) community indifference curve, denoted by A.

This is a simple example of a constrained maximum problem

which can be solved by the usual Lagrange undetermined multiplier technique.

Max.

$$\pi = \pi(\dot{P}, U) \quad \left(\frac{\partial \pi}{\partial \dot{P}}, \frac{\partial \pi}{\partial U} < 0\right) \tag{VIII.3}$$

Subject to

$$\dot{P} - \epsilon - \zeta U^{-1} = 0 \quad (\epsilon < 0, \zeta > 0) \tag{VIII.4}$$

Forming the Lagrange function

$$\pi = \pi(\dot{P}, U) + \lambda \, (\dot{P} - \epsilon - \zeta U^{-1})$$

and setting its partial derivatives equal to zero, the solution is

$$\frac{\partial \pi / \partial U}{\partial \pi / \partial \dot{P}} = \frac{\zeta}{U^2} \tag{VIII.5}$$

However, this 'best-in-an-imperfect-world' solution is not attained automatically. Given the familiar macroeconomic explanation of the working of a market economy, economic fluctuations would be reflected in continuing movement along the 'opportunity slope' so that, in the absence of government intervention, it would be pure chance if the system settled for any length of time at A. Keynesian purists, indeed, would argue that if the system were stuck, say, at B, in underemployment equilibrium there would be no guarantee that intervention in the form of monetary policy would be able to shift the system towards A. Thus the task of fiscal policy is to regulate purchasing power in such a way as to reach A, and *to keep it there,* assuming the community's preference system remains unchanged.

The task of the government economists is to specify the relationship between the change in the budget parameters and the change in the price level and unemployment. The link between the latter, the policy variables, and the former, the policy instruments, is implicit in the analysis in Chapter IV. There we show that the link is a strong one, if Keynesian-type assumptions are realistic, i.e. if the marginal product of labour equals the average product of labour and the wage rate remains constant up to the defined level of full employment of labour. These particular assumptions, as already pointed out (see page 68), assume no trade-off between the level of employment (unemployment) and the price level, if labour is the only variable cost of production. We cannot simply insert equation IV.7 in a suitably modified form at this stage in order to establish the link; i.e. an increase in N is equivalent to a fall in U so that

$$\frac{-dU}{dG} = \left[\frac{1}{1 - b(1 - t_y)}\right] \epsilon \qquad \text{(VIII.6)}$$

We have therefore to take account of the fact that the Phillips curve states that a decrease in U must be associated with an increase in P, so that ϵ, for example, can no longer be regarded as a constant.

It can be accepted that if the economy is below the acceptable rate of unemployment, then an increase in aggregate demand will produce an increase in output and reduce unemployment but 'at the cost of' some increase in P, as specified by the Phillips curve. Therefore we may write

$U = U(Q)$ where $U_Q < 0$
$Q = Q(Y)$ where $Q_y > 0$
$Y = Y(G, t_y)$ where $Y_G > 0, Y_{t_y} < 0$

G = expenditure on goods and services by government where t_y = 'the' tax rate.

It would follow that the usual conclusions regarding fiscal policy would obtain, but in a modified form. Increasing government expenditure would reduce unemployment and decreasing it would increase unemployment and vice versa for a change in 'the' tax rate.

One interesting point emerges from this analysis. As we have seen in Chapter IV, if we alter the 'mix' of taxes between taxes on income and taxes on consumption, we may get changes in the price level which are independent of those caused by changes in the wage rate or the marginal productivity of labour (cf. equation IV.8). Let us consider a situation in which the initial conditions for optimization were satisfied, but for some policy reason it was decided to maintain the same level of aggregate demand, but with a rise in the rate of consumption taxes balanced by a fall in the rate of income tax. (This is, of course, tantamount to introducing an additional constraint, which might reflect government policy on income distribution.) With no shift in Y, there would be no shift in Q or in U, but the price level would rise with the rise in t_i. There would then be an upward shift in the Phillips curve in Figure VIII.1. This is perhaps a healthy reminder that, whatever the origins of the Phillips curve as a statistically observed relationship, we have to treat it as a logical construct in this context. In any case, several writers have cast doubt on the desirability of its 'hold' on the economics profession because of the difficulty in squaring its empirical foundation with several of the influential hypotheses of economic behaviour.

Speculation in recent years has centred on the possibility of shifting the curve to the left, through the use of an appropriate incomes policy. In this context, we assume that this is possible, and can use the opportunity to illustrate once again the problem of co-ordination of fiscal policy with the use of other policy instruments.

A new curve, L', is drawn to the left of the original one, L, which denotes that, for a given fiscal policy, $\dot{P}$ can be held at a lower value for a given level of unemployment. If fiscal policy remains unchanged, the point C is attained which is preferred to A. The interesting point, however, is that this is not the optimal situation, for the community would prefer to be at A' rather than C with a lower level of unemployment and a higher $\dot{P}$. The result of the (successful!) operation of an incomes policy means that fiscal parameters must be changed to adjust the system to reach A'. In short, this offers again a useful illustration of Bent Hansen's important point that attainment of given ends presupposes an optimal mix of policies and therefore co-ordination between the various authorities responsible for them.

A word of warning is necessary at this stage of the analysis, and may bear repeating at a later stage. It is comparatively easy to add to the number of policy instruments which might be brought to bear on the shape and location of the opportunity slope. In any policy situation, however, it would be naive to assume that the choice of policy instruments did not affect the social welfare function. In the above example, an incomes policy may very well achieve a shift in the opportunity slope, as represented by the Phillips curve, but its distributional effects may require us to add another dimension to the social welfare function. Put another way, the social indifference system may not remain stable throughout the process of adjustment from point A to C to A', in which case it will be impossible to say whether or not the new policy 'mix' has improved social welfare.

III. EXAMPLE 2: GROWTH AND CONSUMPTION

Let us assume that the two elements in the social welfare function are growth and consumption defined in the following way:

$(dY/dn) \cdot (1/Y) = y$ where y is the percentage rate of growth in a period of time;

$C/Y \qquad = x$ where x is the proportion of national output devoted to consumption.

It is further assumed that the 'trade-off' between y and x can be represented by the usual set of indifference curves denoting the declining social utility of growth with respect to consumption. We may also add in two constraints. There is some minimum 'tolerable' percentage of output to be devoted to consumption, e.g. a subsistence minimum, and some minimum 'tolerable' growth rate, perhaps because a growth rate below that level would result in an 'intolerable' level of unemployment given a growing labour force.

We can now write our social welfare function as

$$\pi = \pi(x, y)$$

where $\pi_x, \pi_y > 0$. \hfill (VIII. 7)

The next stage of our analysis is to identify the production relations in the economy which will enable us to determine the 'opportunity line' relating growth and consumption. Clearly, it is reasonable to suppose that a community which sacrifices consumption at the margin can have a higher rate of growth, abstracting from problems associated with maintaining full employment of resources and the terms of trade between the relevant country and its trading partners. Let us assume that there is no problem about maintaining the level of aggregate demand sufficient to produce full employment of resources and that the economy is a closed one.

One such relation between sacrifice of consumption and increase in growth is implicit in our previous Harrod-Domar growth model, namely that for a given level of *ex ante* investment (= *ex ante* saving) and ICOR, we can predict the rate of growth of the

Fiscal Policy and Constrained Maximization

economy. In order to avoid problems associated with the dependence of output on the growth of the labour force, we can assume that capital and labour are employed in fixed proportions and that, for any values of y and x in the welfare function, there is no labour constraint. We can achieve the optimum rate of growth (as later determined) without fear of labour shortage.

We can now write our simple production function as

$$\frac{dY}{dn} \cdot \frac{1}{Y} = \frac{\dot{Y}}{Y} = y = \frac{1}{\phi} \cdot \rho \qquad \text{(VIII. 8)}$$

where $\phi = \text{ICOR} = 1/h$ and is assumed constant (i.e. $\phi = \bar{\phi}$)

$\rho = I/Y = $ proportion of investment to GNP.

There is no depreciation of capital, so that gross investment equals net investment.

If the economy has no problems in reaching the warranted rate of growth path, $I_n/Y_n = S_n/Y_n = 1 - (C_n/Y_n)$ for all n. It follows that we can write

$$C/Y = x = 1 - \rho \qquad \text{(VIII. 9)}$$

and from equation VIII. 8, as $y\bar{\phi} = \rho$, expression VIII. 9 can be rewritten as

$$x = 1 - \bar{\phi}y \qquad \text{(VIII. 9a)}$$

We now have a social welfare function, which can be maximized, subject to the 'production constraint'

$$\pi = \pi(x, y)$$

where $\pi_x, \pi_y > 0$ and subject to equation VIII. 9a.

Using the Lagrange multiplier we obtain

$$\Pi = \pi(x, y) + \lambda(1 - \bar{\phi}y - x)$$

$$\Pi_x = \pi_x - \lambda = 0 \qquad \text{(VIII. 10a)}$$

$$\Pi_y = \pi_y - \lambda\bar{\phi} = 0 \qquad \text{(VIII. 10b)}$$

$$\Pi_\lambda = 1 - \bar{\phi}y - x = 0 \qquad \text{(VIII. 10c)}$$

Substituting in equation VIII. 10a we have

$$\pi_x - \frac{\pi_y}{\bar{\phi}} = 0 \text{ or } \frac{\pi_x}{\pi_y} = \frac{1}{\bar{\phi}}$$

As before, we can express our results in graphical form as in Figure VIII. 2. The indifference curves are given the usual shape,

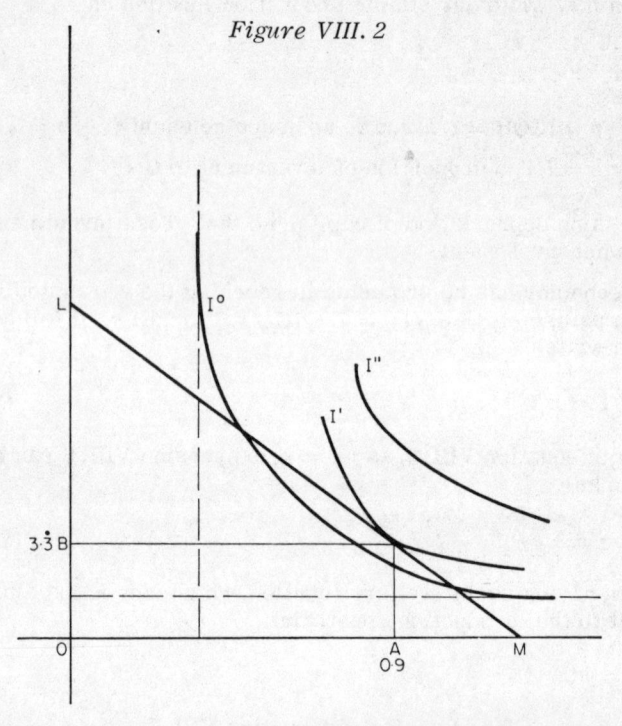

Figure VIII. 2

and the slope of the opportunity line LM *must be equal to the value of the ICOR*, for $dx/dy = -\bar{\phi}$. The optimal position is by definition that point where I' touches the opportunity line. Therefore, with $\bar{\phi} = 3$, and the optimal consumption level, i.e. $x = 0.9$ (OA), then solving for y in equation VIII. 9a gives us a rate of growth of 3·33 per cent per annum (OB).

Although the example used assumes a constant ICOR, this is not a necessary restrictive assumption. If we assume a variable ICOR, e.g. ϕ, we can rewrite $x = 1 - [f(\phi)]y$ so that $dx/dy = -f(\phi)$. The opportunity line then becomes concave to the origin.

Fiscal Policy and Constrained Maximization

There is no reason to suppose that the economic system would automatically achieve the optimal position, as determined by the shape of the social welfare function, any more than, in our previous example, it would achieve exactly the optimal trade-off between the rate of changes in prices and the unemployment rate. This is not to say that we have any *technical* means of choosing whether or not a 'non-interventionist' situation, with, say, a lower rate of growth and higher consumption rate, is any better or worse than another trade-off which requires fiscal intervention. It is sufficient for our purpose to know that governments in practice frequently carry out policies, often in response to popular demand, to intervene.

The policy question is, therefore, how to move the economy along the opportunity line, or possibly to adjust the slope of the line itself, in order to optimize, given the social welfare function. It is conceivable that there may be fiscal policies which could lower the value of ϕ and therefore 'swivel' the line to the right, starting from point A. For the moment, let us concentrate on the ways in which the government can alter the investment rate, ρ, by fiscal means, it being the only remaining independent variable in the production function.

Having already assumed that there is no policy problem about maintaining full employment of resources, in the sense that an increase in aggregate saving will not reduce consumption to the level where there will be excess capacity caused by lack of effective demand, we can view the policy task as that of releasing resources for investment purposes by the use of the budget. Raising the level of aggregate saving by fiscal means is an obvious way of obtaining this release of resources, as already explained in Chapter V, for the government can influence the rate of private and public saving by adjustments in tax rates and government expenditure rates. This can be demonstrated very simply by equating ρ with government saving (the excess of taxes [less transfers] over current expenditure on goods and services) and private saving (the excess of personal income [less taxes] over personal expenditure on current goods and services). We neglect business saving. Then

$$\rho = \frac{I}{Y} = \frac{sY(1-t_y)}{Y} + \frac{(t_y - g) Y}{Y}$$

where s = proportion of personal income saved, $\quad 0 < s < 1$
t_y = 'the' tax rate— a proportional tax on income, $\quad 0 < t_y < 1$

g = proportion of real national product devoted to government expenditure on current goods and services, $\quad 0 < g < 1$

More simply still,

$$\rho = \frac{I}{Y} = s(1 - t_y) + (t_y - g)$$

We obtain the familiar conclusion that, pound for pound, lowering the rate of government spending, g, is a more effective means of raising the investment ratio, ρ, than raising the tax rate, t_y. This follows from the proposition that, whereas t_y raises the *ex ante* budget surplus (or reduces the deficit), it also reduces disposable incomes and, by our assumptions, also reduces the level of private savings. The converse is also true.

As in the previous example, the reader must be warned that it is one thing to indicate the way in which the theory of economic policy explains the role of fiscal policy in maximizing some community welfare function, but it is another thing to draw precise conclusions applicable to any particular situation. The point may be illustrated by considering the use of a change in t_y as a means of optimizing the welfare function. On the one hand, a rise in t_y may affect the level of growth not only through its effect on raising the level of saving which 'permits' the higher investment rate which is assumed to be necessary in order to optimize; it is conceivable that it could also lower the growth rate through its effect on the incentives to work. Therefore, the opportunity slope itself may shift as a result of the use of a particular policy instrument. Again, a change in the tax rate which produced changes in the distribution of income might lead the community, through its representatives, to consider that the welfare function had not been correctly specified, or that a 'distributional constraint' had not been taken into account. Although this warning is needed, it does point to one useful feature of even a simplified exposition of the theory of economic policy, namely the emphasis it lays on having explicit information about the nature of the objective function, and all the relevant information about the constraints which govern the process of maximizing it.

IV. EXAMPLE 3: EMPLOYMENT CREATION IN DEVELOPING ECONOMIES

Our final example of constrained maximization is that of employment creation within the developing economies. This implies a departure from our former analysis in that hitherto, when discussing employment policies, we have explicitly adopted a Keynesian framework. That is to say, we have normally assumed that when resources are unemployed an increase in aggregate monetary demand will stimulate an expansion of physical output and raise the numbers of those engaged in productive employment. The essential assumption underlying Keynesian policies to alleviate unemployment is that supply conditions are elastic. Low levels of output are the consequences solely of a lack of effective demand and raising the level of aggregate demand—by either reducing taxation, raising government expenditures, or extending credit—is indicated as the appropriate remedy.

One of the more interesting questions in present-day economics is whether such a conceptual framework is applicable to the problems confronting the 'developing economies'. Our interest is mainly in those economies with extensive unemployment—either open or disguised—which are often referred to as the surplus labour economies. It is generally conceded that the existence of such unemployment with all its attendant social and political difficulties cannot be tolerated, particularly with regard to the induced inflow of agrarian unemployed to the urban areas.

It is commonly argued that under these conditions Keynesian policies are inapplicable in the attempt to expand employment opportunities. Unemployment is seen as the consequence, not of a deficiency of effective demand, but rather of an excess of labour in relation to the available capital stock which imposes a limit to the permissible level of output. The capacity level of output is attained long before the labour force is fully utilized. Under these conditions an increase in aggregate monetary demand would merely be inflationary and exacerbate balance of payments difficulties. This situation is summarized in the composite diagram of Figure VIII.3. Part (a) depicts a conventional Keynesian increase in aggregate monetary expenditures. In Part (b) the monetary level of national income is translated into real terms by the aggregate supply function whilst the lower portion of the figure shows the output-employment relationship and the extent of unemployment. Finally, Part (c) of the figure gives the relationship between aggregate monetary demand and the price level (drawn for any given capacity of real income) and postulates an assumed relationship between the price level and imports.[2]

It is Part (b) of the figure which sums up the case against the use of Keynesian policies in the less advanced economies. Here the

Figure VIII.3

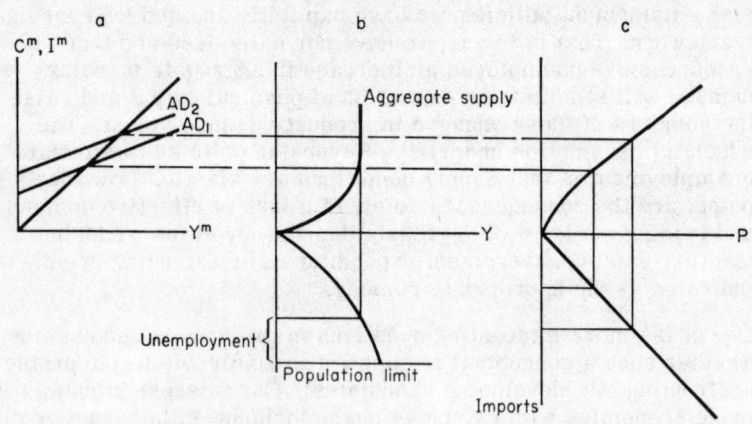

![Figure VIII.3: Three-panel diagram. Panel a shows C^m, I^m vs Y^m with AD₁ and AD₂ curves. Panel b shows Aggregate supply vs Y with Unemployment and Population limit marked. Panel c shows Imports vs P.]

inelastic portion of the aggregate supply curve is attained long before the full employment level of the labour force is reached. In contrast, in the advanced industrial economy, the causal relationship is usually reversed. It is the attainment of full employment of the labour force which imposes a limit to the sustainable output level and may lead to balance of payments problems.

Whether the less advanced economies face such supply limitations must remain an empirical issue which cannot be determined *a priori*. Even if supply conditions are more elastic than has usually been supposed, the application of standard Keynesian remedies may not necessarily be appropriate or capable of being carried out. For example, it is sometimes argued that there is frequently excess capacity in manufacturing industry in developing countries and that in consequence both output and employment could be increased, i.e. there is no trade-off problem between output and employment, if demand were increased for manufacturing products by some form of fiscal action. It turns out that this is quite a complex analytical and policy problem. In this context, it will be sufficient to illustrate the complexities by showing how much information would need to be in the hands of the fiscal authorities, if suitable action were contemplated.

Consider the case in which the fiscal measure used to increase output is a straight output subsidy, and the supply curves of the relevant industries subsidized are completely elastic over the relevant range. In addition there is another set of 'industries', e.g. agriculture and services, whose supply curves are completely inelastic (a strong assumption of course) in the short run. The direction of the changes which will result from such fiscal action and the consequent 'side effects' will be as follows:

1. The 'first-round effect' of a subsidy will appear to be an increase in output and demand for labour, but the *extent* of the increase will depend on the price elasticity of demand for manufacturing goods. Even if the effect is positive, an increase in the demand for labour does not necessarily lead to an increase in the demand for numbers employed. The assumption that all labour is homogeneous is implicit in the suggestion that raising the demand for labour means an increase in numbers employed, whereas the actual situation in developing countries may be nearer one in which there are shortages of skilled labour for manufacturing. Therefore, even if the first-round effect means that demand for labour increases, much more needs to be known about the nature of the labour input required, as well as labour-hiring policies generally, before any conclusion can be drawn.

2. The 'second-round effects' can be dichotomized into various injections and leakages. The rise in total output will cause a corresponding rise in *incomes* with consequential positive multiplier effects which feed back through consumption expenditure to increase demand for both agricultural and manufacturing products. The fiscal authorities clearly have to know what the income elasticities of demand are for the various sectors, both in order to know whether the changes are having the desired effects and, incidentally, in order to be able to calculate the required amount of subsidy. If we assume equi-proportional consumption in the two sectors, then all demand curves will move to the right. In the case of manufacturing, by assumption, output and demand for labour input will further increase. In the case of the other sectors, again by assumption, the effect will be a rise in prices; i.e. the domestic 'terms of trade' will move in favour of these sectors.

3. There are similar effects, which have to be calculated in the case of the changes in demand produced through the inter-industry system. One effect of interdependency in the economy is that agricultural inputs for industry will rise in price, so that the output-promoting effects of the subsidy to manufacturing will be offset by the rise in variable costs. Another is that leakages will 'soften' the domestic impact of the subsidy change, provided that the tax system is flexible enough to 'pick up' revenue as domestic output expands, e.g. through corporation taxes and income tax collected at source, and also provided that imports are allowed

to expand. Again, measurement requires a calculation of the income elasticity of both taxes and demand for imports.

4. There will be further effects which are not discernible in the input-output system. These will increase: (i) the effects on demand and on the general price level of the change in relative prices of manufactured and other goods and services; (ii) the effects on the economy of the alternative methods of financing the subsidy which are open to the government.

Now let us review the use of fiscal policy to create employment in the circumstances just described, bearing in mind the kind of policy context we have in mind. *Firstly*, it is not certain *a priori* that employment in terms of labour units will increase, so that much more needs to be known about the nature of the industrial conditions obtaining in any particular developing country before one can be sure that fiscal instruments will achieve the desired aim. *Secondly*, there is quite a long list of assumptions to be formulated and tested in order to analyse both the direction and magnitude of change. An input-output table for the economy is essential, but the use of such a table is limited by the assumption of proportionality in the inter-industry system, an assumption which it is not possible to make when the very nature of the situation we are interested in requires differing elasticities of supply. *Thirdly*, even if the full effects on employment and the side effects can be calculated, the degree of 'fine tuning' in the fiscal system necessary to produce the desired result while minimizing the side effects is almost certainly not possible in many developing countries.

If it is conceded that supply conditions are inelastic so that policies to promote employment are not accompanied by any notable increase in physical output, then we are at once faced with a cruel dilemma, for attempts at employment creation will normally entail less efficient modes of production than would otherwise obtain; this is particularly true of the public sector. If the public sector is deliberately made more labour-intensive in order to raise employment levels it is reasonable to conclude that the per-unit cost of output will thereby be raised. As long as the government sector faces a budget constraint, the implication must be that employment creation policies will be accompanied by a decrease in total output. Indeed, this conclusion is implicit in the attempt to depart from the factor-mix combination determined by profit-maximizing motives in the private sector. It follows that, the more that resources are transferred from the private to the public sector, the greater will be the level of employment but the lower will be total output; per capita income must fall. We have a clear example of trade-off which we summarize in Figure VIII. 4.

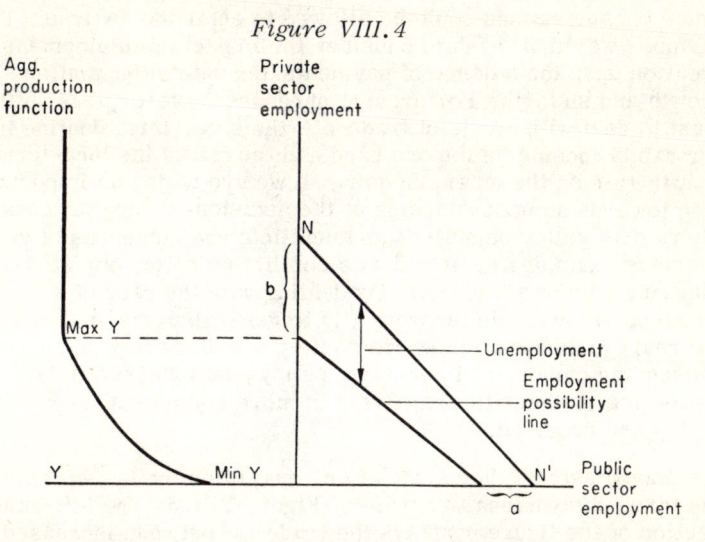

Figure VIII.4

In Figure VIII. 4, the line NN' represents the total population which may seek employment in either the public or the private sector. National income is maximized when all employed resources are allocated solely in the private sector but extensive unemployment results, indicated by b. Unemployment is minimized, a, by a policy of transferring all employable resources to the public sector. $b > a$, but this also implies the minimal income level. The nature of the trade-off is simply the extent to which national income must be given up in order to obtain an increment to the total numbers employed.

However, the question of trade-off is more complex than this. The cost of employment creation will in all probability involve a decrease in the rate of growth. This follows from a number of considerations. Firstly, the decline in the level of per capita income will normally reduce the pace of capital formation. This will be reinforced if labour-intensive methods of production increase the percentage of resources flowing to labour and away from the owners of capital and if saving propensities differ between the respective income classes.[3] Secondly, quite apart from any adverse impacts upon capital formation, the adoption of more labour-intensive methods may slow the pace of technological change since the latter is generally associated with an increase in the amount of capital per capita.

Other considerations could be allowed to enter the analysis. For example, we might wish to consider the impact of employment creation upon the balance of payments, the rate of population growth and so forth. For present purposes, however, it is sufficient to deal with our joint trade-off—the short-term decline in per capita income on the one hand and the fall in the long-term growth rate on the other. In doing so we are taking an important step towards an understanding of the decision-making process where both policy objectives and conflicts are numerous. Our previous examples dealt with two conflicting policy objectives implying only one trade-off. By dealing with the case of a multiple trade-off we are able theoretically to generalize the analysis to the real-world situation where society's welfare function encompasses any number of interacting policy goals and conflicts. Whilst the mathematical analysis is more complex no new principles are required.

We may illustrate the nature of our dual dilemma by reference to the three-dimensional diagram of Figure VIII.5. The left-hand section of the figure portrays the trade-off between increased employment and income per capita, whilst the right-hand segment depicts a similar situation between increased employment and economic growth. The solid thus described shows all possible combinations of higher employment, per capita income and long-term economic growth. We may imagine a series of community indifference curves emanating from the origin and progressively slicing the solid until a tangency solution between the community indifference curve and the conical surface is attained. Any further indifference curve is theoretically unattainable. The tangency solution maximizes the welfare of society. We may carry the analysis a stage further, however, by postulating a minimum level of income per capita which is politically acceptable and likewise by assuming a minimal growth rate which is deemed feasible in the light of all other conditions. The two are, of course, interrelated in that a rate of growth of income in excess of population expansion automatically leads to a raising of income per capita and vice versa.

Let us assume that the minimal level of income per capita is given by $\bar{y}$, and the lowest acceptable rate of growth by $\bar{z}$. Lower values of y and z are inadmissible when we are considering the social welfare function. Alternatively, we may say that minimal values are imposed upon the constraints which then delimit the feasible range of policy action.

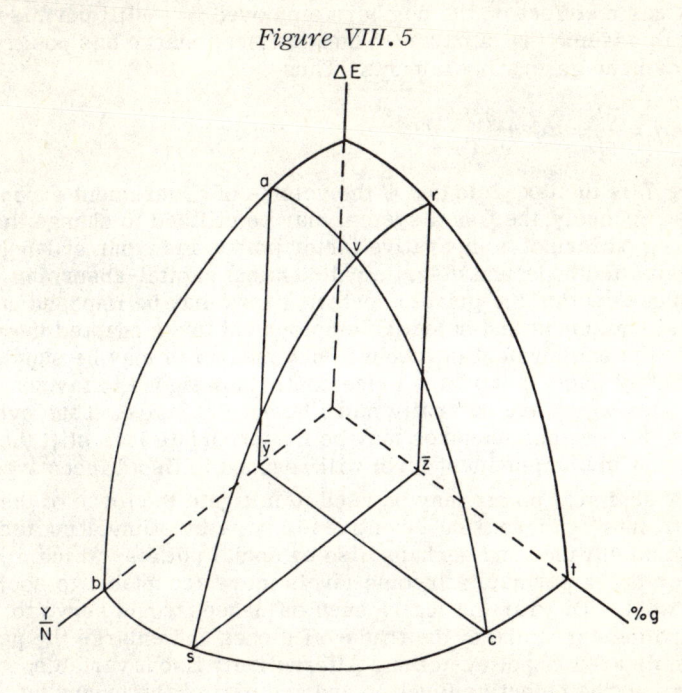

Figure VIII.5

The effect of imposing the minimal income level, $\bar{y}$, reduces the permissible surface of the solid to the area abc. Likewise the impact of adopting a minimal growth rate, $\bar{z}$, implies that only the surface rst is available to policy action. The combined constraint thus reduces the scope of permissible policy action to the area vsc.

More formally, our objective function is represented by

$$u = u(N, y, z)$$

where u is again the ordinal utility index and is maximized subject to the dual constraint $y \geq \bar{y}$ and $z \geq \bar{z}$.

Now that we have indicated the nature of the problem, what is the scope for fiscal policy? Firstly, as we have already shown, once the decision has been taken to render the public sector more labour-intensive, enlarging the size of the public sector *vis-à-vis* the private sector will raise the aggregate numbers employed. Thus even though an increase in aggregate monetary demand by itself has no effect on the numbers employed it is still permissible to assume that a balanced budget fiscal change has positive employment-generating impacts. Thus

$$dN = \frac{\partial N}{\partial G} \cdot dG + \frac{\partial N}{\partial T} \cdot dT > 0$$

where T is the tax yield and G the volume of government expenditures. Secondly, the fiscal system may be utilized to change the existing pattern of comparative factor prices in favour of labour-intensive methods, and discriminate against capital-absorbing techniques within the private sector. Taxes may be imposed upon capital equipment and selective employment taxes adapted to subsidize the employment of labour. Such measures may be supplemented by wage, import and price controls designed to favour activities which are naturally more labour-intensive. Thus even though Keynesian measures may be inappropriate it is still the case that the employment level will respond to fiscal incentives.

Likewise, fiscal policy may be used to mitigate the force of the constraints by increasing incentives to save, by stimulating technological advance and perhaps also by social policies which render lower per capita income levels more acceptable to society as a whole. Diagrammatically, such influences would serve to change the curvature of the trade-off slopes and enlarge the permissible area of policy action. Alternatively fiscal variables enter into the objective function and are part of the means by which the utility index is maximized. We do not need to pursue the now familiar technique of the Lagrange multiplier to determine the outcome; without specifying the functional relationships more precisely we are not able to advance the analysis beyond our diagrammatic framework.

We do not mean to simplify the tremendous problems facing the emergent nations by suggesting that fiscal policy may solve all difficulties; all that we have proposed in the present example is that fiscal variables must be given due notice in the maximization procedure. Our purpose in the present illustration has been to show that the question of decision-making need not be confined to a Keynesian framework and that neither is it confined to a dual objective policy problem. Goals, conflicts, and instruments are manifold. The purpose of the present volume has been merely to

Fiscal Policy and Constrained Maximization 157

indicate the place and importance of the fiscal variable in the complex schema of economic decision making.

V. INTER-TEMPORAL UTILITY MAXIMIZATION AND FISCAL POLICY

Thus far our analysis of the use of fiscal policy in maximizing a social welfare function has assumed that we are interested in some terminal position which, given the shape of the utility function, the boundary conditions and technical constraints, is the best conceivable. Time does not enter into the utility function or into the examination of the process of adjustment of the fiscal system to reach the 'bliss' point. We have shown in Chapter V that the introduction of time and the introduction of lagged responses in the system modify policy prescriptions. It seems worth investigating how far lagged responses also complicate the whole question of community choices with regard to both objectives and instruments.

Let us use a very simple example. Let us assume that a particular fiscal 'mix' of taxes and expenditures obtains which results in a growth pattern of national output depicted by curve A_1 in Figure VIII.6. The substitution of another 'mix' produces an alternative pattern which is represented by curve A_2. Which is the 'better' mix? To answer this question, the economist must ask the policy maker a series of questions:

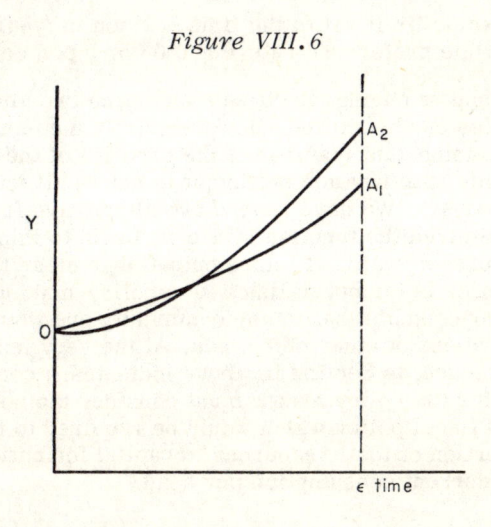

Figure VIII.6

(a) What is the nature of the objective function? Is the policy maker interested solely in growth in national output or are other objectives to be considered? Let us assume for the moment that the answer is that the policy maker is interested solely in growth.

(b) Curve A_1 produces more output in the near future as compared with A_2, but less in the future. How does the policy maker view output as a function of time? The accepted way of comparing present with future utilities is, of course, to select some discount rate, and it would be reasonable to assume that this rate is positive denoting that the present value of a unit of output in the future is less than the present value of a unit of output now.

(c) What time horizon is relevant? The policy maker may have no interest in the effects of fiscal policy in the remote future when he may not be in office, or when changes in the shape of the objective function take place. In other words, after some point in time the value of future output is nil, i.e. the rate of discount is infinite, and to compare present with future output we must assume that the objective or utility function is stable.

We can now specify the objective function as follows:

$$\pi_0(Y_i) = \sum_{n=1}^{\epsilon} \frac{\pi_n(Y_i)}{(1+i)^n}$$

where ϵ is some limit set to the time horizon in 'years'; $0 < i < 1$ is a social time preference rate, e.g. 0·05 or 5 per cent.

The policy maker having specified n and i, the two alternative fiscal policies can be ranked. However, while the example illustrates some important features of the problem of the choice of fiscal policies in a dynamic setting, it is not on all fours with the previous analysis. We have *ranked* two alternative fiscal policies, but not maximized the function. Once we begin to think of maximizing the present value of future output, it is clear that the objective function is far out of line with a policy-making situation, for it is inconceivable that in any community one would maximize output regardless of other objectives. At the very least, one would want to introduce, as Section III above indicates, a consumption constraint, for the policy maker must consider the social implications of a fiscal policy which would be required to transfer a large proportion of total resources to capital formation at the expense of current consumption per head.

The example chosen is merely illustrative. In actual planning models which fix the pattern of thinking about policy problems, particularly in developing countries, an attempt is made to grapple with the problems of the real world by devising much more complicated objective functions, and using multi-sector growth models of a high degree of sophistication, all within a dynamic framework. The reader must take it on trust that even an exercise in comparative statics involving only two time periods, a simple two-sector growth model and two 'arguments' (i.e. the 'O.K.' terminology for the elements in the objective function) requires the use of mathematical techniques which are beyond the scope of this work, and also lead us into untrodden ways so far as the fiscal economists are concerned. Until public finance has come more to terms with these new developments, we can avoid troubling the reader with a further input of economic theory with a (fairly) clear conscience.[4]

NOTES

[1] The reader will recall the discussion in Chapter IV of the relation between prices, employment and output, and our emphasis on the special assumptions used in the Keynesian model, which assumes no trade-off between employment and price level.

[2] I.e. that the cross-elasticity between imports and domestic goods is positive.

[3] Although consideration of the Cobb-Douglas production function would suggest that greater labour intensity would not change the respective income shares of labour and capital. This, however, is to assume all adjustments are frictionless and to ignore any short-term deviations from the long-term ultimate solution.

[4] The interested (and mathematically versatile) reader may obtain a taste of these complications by consulting Louis Lefeber, 'Planning in a Surplus Labour Economy', *American Economic Review*, Vol. LVIII, June 1968. This article makes specific reference to the use of tax/subsidy policy for increasing employment in developing countries.

Chapter IX

FISCAL POLICY AND UNCERTAINTY: AN INTRODUCTION

I. INTRODUCTION

So far the 'policy rules' which would follow from the analysis simply depend on the postulated relationships in the model considered appropriate to the economy we are interested in and to the social welfare or objective function. In the special case where the government wishes to achieve particular target values of variables in the model, it has been demonstrated that the government needs only as many instruments, represented by variables in the model under its control, as there are targets. It follows that if all the relevant variables are contained in the model, their interrelations correctly specified, and the values of the parameters correctly estimated, then policy optimization begins to look like an exercise in rather simple mathematics. If mistakes are made in the optimization process, they must arise from misunderstanding between the policy maker and economist, e.g. about the targets or trade-offs, or the 'boundary conditions' placed on instruments, or from errors in algebra or in computation. An important question arises when we can no longer assume that the response by target variables or arguments in the social welfare function to changes in policy instruments is known for certain. Even in an abstract work of this kind, it would be foolish to ignore the fact that no policy maker lives in a world of certainty, in the sense of knowing exactly what the effect of the magnitude of change in, say, some fiscal instrument will be on some particular target variable, such as the level of national income. Even if we abstract from uncertainties surrounding policy makers' own preferences, the selection of the relevant variables whose relationships are depicted in a model may be faulty, so that even directions of change may be wrongly specified. *A fortiori*, even if the directions of change are correctly discerned governments are interested in magnitudes of change, which raises the further difficulty, *inter alia*, that values of parameters may be incorrectly forecasted.

A simple example will both explain the difficulties facing policy makers and help us to form an agenda for further discussion.

Fiscal Policy and Uncertainty: an Introduction

Equation II.2 can be rewritten in the simplified form,

$$Y = \overline{A}k + \overline{G}k + \overline{I}k \qquad (IX.1)$$

where $\overline{A} = \alpha - b(\eta - R)$

$k = 1/(1 - b + bt_y)$ (the multiplier).

Let us assume that the policy makers wish to achieve some given level of Y, call it Y_1, using government expenditure as the instrument. In a certain world, with correct forecasts of the values of A, k and I, Y can be achieved by correct adjustment of G, which is assumed to be under the policy makers' control. But what happens if the forecast of I proves to be wrong? We can illustrate the problem in the familiar simple diagram of first-year economics.

In Figure IX.1, if all other values are correctly forecasted, it is possible that the I forecast may be too high or too low, with the

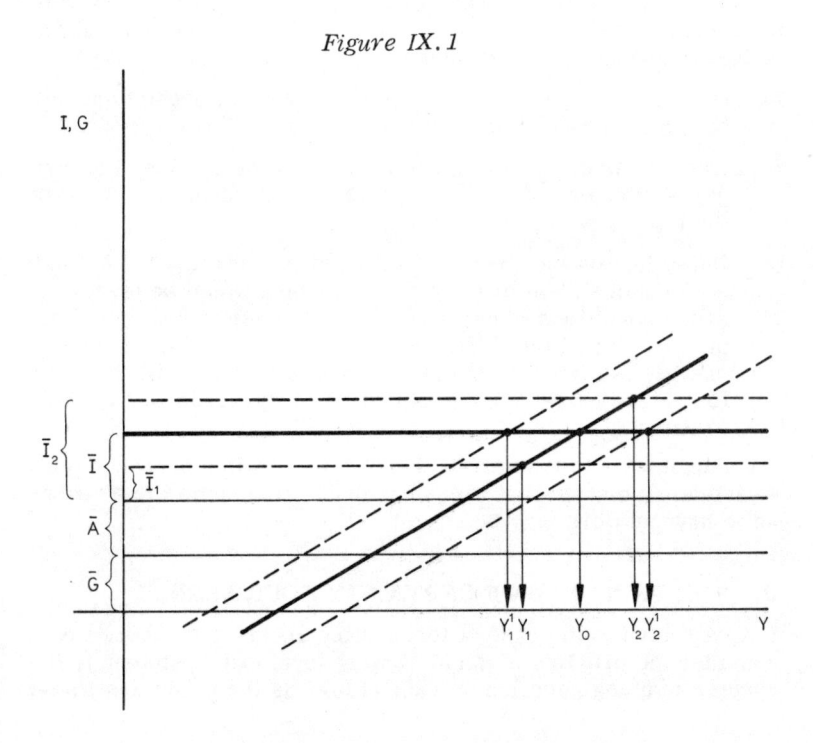

Figure IX.1

consequence that Y will be too high or too low, given the policy objective of a single-valued Y. If the government acts on the assumption of a correct forecast of I, then if actual investment turns out to be I_1 the achieved level of Y will be $Y_1 < Y_0$; similarly, if it turns out to be I_2 the achieved level of Y will be $Y_2 > Y_0$. This may be called an example of *forecasting uncertainty*.

Let us take the example where the exogenous terms are all correctly forecasted but k is not, as would be the case where the marginal propensity to save or consume, b, was incorrectly forecasted. If the forecasted value of b were too low (i.e. the marginal propensities were too high) the achieved level of Y would be lower than required (say Y_1'), and if the forecasted value of b were too high (i.e. the marginal propensities were too low) Y would be higher than required (say Y_2'). In this case the effect of the policy instrument, G, would be uncertain because of the uncertainty attached to the value of k. This may be called an example of *policy uncertainty*.

This problem suggests a number of important questions about the appropriate advice that economists should give to policy makers under conditions of uncertainty:

(a) Is there an appropriate way of attempting to predict uncertain outcomes to policy action?

(b) Are less than 'perfect' results likely to be obtained because of the very existence of uncertainty? How does one evaluate the effects of uncertain outcomes?

(c) Depending on the answers to (a) and (b), how far will optimal policy adjustment differ from that which would be found under conditions of certainty? Will the adjustment rules be affected by: (i) the different sorts of uncertainty, i.e. forecasting as distinct from policy uncertainty, and (ii) the wish to achieve more than one objective or by 'trade-off' considerations?

We cannot hope to answer all these questions in a complete and satisfactory manner, but we can at least offer some illustrations as to how answers may be sought.[1]

II. THE PRINCIPLE OF CERTAINTY EQUIVALENCE

Let us return to the case of forecasting uncertainty where we consider the problem of deciding what level of investment, I, to assume in using government expenditure as the policy instrument

Fiscal Policy and Uncertainty: an Introduction

to achieve the desired level of Y. In the course of applying macroeconomic analysis to policy questions, post mortems on forecasts embodying policy variables may enable one to offer some judgement on the likelihood of investment outcomes in the future. At least it may be possible to narrow down the range of alternative outcomes so that some are worth considering and others are not.

A formal analysis of this procedure is found in what is known as the calculation of the mathematical expectation of a particular event's occurring. Thus uncertainty is often defined in economics as a situation where the probability of a particular event's occurring is considered to be less than 100 per cent. If a is the probability that an investment level of I_1 will occur, then the mathematical expectation of this outcome is aI_1 where $a < 1$. But if this outcome is uncertain then other outcomes, although uncertain, are possible. If we can list all the members of the total set of alternative values of a random variable X and assign each value a probability, a, then the mathematical expectation or expected value of X can be calculated as follows:

$$ME = a_1X_1 + a_2X_2 + \ldots + a_nX_n = \sum_{j=1}^{n} a_jX_j \qquad (\text{IX. 2})$$

$$= \Sigma \, aX$$

as $a_1 + a_2 + \ldots + a_n = 1$. Now $\sum_{j=1}^{u} a_jX_j$ is equivalent to the relative frequency of the occurrence of a particular value of X. We can then write

$$ME = \sum_{j=1}^{n} a_jX_j = \frac{\Sigma f_1(\widetilde{X})}{\Sigma f_j} = \widetilde{X} \qquad (\text{IX. 3})$$

In other words, the mathematical expectation or the expected outcome, $\widetilde{X}$, is equal to the *mean* of the total population of outcomes, where the probability weights, the a_s, are equivalent to the relative frequencies of their occurrence. Reverting to our previous example, if we identify only two outcomes of expected levels of investment I_1 and I_2, with forecasted values of 25 and 30 and probabilities of $3/5$ and $2/5$ respectively, then

$$ME = 3/5 \cdot 25 + 2/5 \cdot 30 = 27$$

(To check whether this equals the mean value, express the probabilities in percentage terms, so that $\widetilde{X} = (60/100)25 + (40/100)30 = 27$).

Does the choice of the mean of uncertain outcomes offer a useful decision rule in circumstances where there is uncertainty? The answer, as we shall see, crucially depends upon the valuation placed by policy makers on deviations from the desired outcome or, in other words, upon the attitude towards uncertaintly adopted by them which is reflected in the objective function. This point may be illustrated with reference to the example in Figure IX.1, with the addition of a very special kind of objective function.

The desired value of national income, Y_0, represented an *optimum optimorum*, but because of the possibility of forecasting uncertainty it may not be achieved. The deviation from the desired value is then given by the expression

$$[Y_0 - k(\overline{I} + \overline{G})]^2$$

where $Y = k(\overline{I} + \overline{G})$. (We shall ignore the expression $k\overline{A}$ for simplicity.) Thus a simple form of quadratic objective function is assumed in which policy makers assume that positive and negative deviations from Y_0 have equal disutility and disutility is measured by the square of the deviations from the optimum optimorum. The objective function, u, can now be defined thus:

$$u = -[Y_0 - k(\overline{I} + \overline{G})]^2 \tag{IX.4}$$

Now let us assume, as before, that I_1 and I_2 are the only possible investment outcomes, investment being exogenously determined, and that all other values can be correctly forecasted. Following the procedure suggested by the analysis of mathematical expectation we can rewrite the objective function in terms of the expected disutility derived from deviations from the desired value of Y, i.e. Y_0:

$$u_e = -a_1[Y_0 - k(\overline{I_1} + \overline{G})]^2 - a_2[Y_0 - k(\overline{I_2} + \overline{G})]^2 \tag{IX.5}$$

where $a_1 + a_2 = 1$ and therefore $a_2 = 1 - a_1$. In order to determine which value of $\overline{G}$ should be chosen in order to minimize this expression, we differentiate u_e with respect to G and set the result equal to zero—following the normal maximization rule. It is then found that

$$k[\overline{I_1}a_1 + \overline{I_2}(1 - a_1)] - Y_0 + k\overline{G} = 0 \tag{IX.6}$$

Fiscal Policy and Uncertainty: an Introduction

Following our previous analysis, the expression in square brackets is equivalent to the expected value of I, i.e. $\bar{I}$, so that expression IX. 6 may be rewritten

$$k\tilde{I} - Y_0 + k\overline{G} = 0 \text{ or } \overline{G} = \frac{Y_0}{k} - \tilde{I} \tag{IX. 7}$$

It can easily be seen that there is only one difference between the decision rules for equations IX. 1 and IX. 7, in respect of $\overline{G}$. In equation IX. 1, $\overline{G}$ is adjusted to achieve Y_0 for correctly known values of $\overline{I}$ and k. In equation IX. 7, the decision rule becomes: choose that value of $\overline{G}$ which will achieve Y_0 *as if the expected value of $\overline{I}$ were equal to the actual value*; this is known as invoking the *principle of certainty equivalence*.

We have illustrated the development of rules for action under conditions of uncertainty using a simple one-target, one-instrument approach. The model which we have used, however, contains two fiscal instruments, $\overline{G}$ and also t_y (the rate of income tax). Unless there are policy constraints placed on their use, e.g. a restriction on the size of the government budget relative to the GNP, the simple static model offers no instructions about the relative merits of using one instrument rather than another. More complex models embodying more than one target, with lags and other features, may offer more specific advice, and there may be a host of practical reasons why in a particular country at a particular time one instrument may be preferred to another. However, let us for the moment stick to our simple model, but concentrate on the problem of uncertainty as before. It will be demonstrated that our simple probabilistic approach requires further development if, given alternative courses of policy action, the range of uncertainty differs with each course.

As before, we invite the policy maker to fix a target level of Y, and we assume that if we use $\overline{G}$ as the instrument the uncertainty attached to the forecast value of $\overline{I}$ can be represented as before. If, alternatively, it is decided to leave the level of $\overline{G}$ unaltered and to alter t_y, this in effect alters the value of k for, given the usual assumptions, $k = 1/(1 - b + bt_y)$. By altering k the values of the expressions $k\overline{G}$ and $k\overline{I}$ are both altered. To make the analysis even simpler, let us assume that the government correctly forecasts its own expenditure on goods and services. We are left with the problem of the uncertainty attached to the possible investment outcomes when t_y is altered. If we followed the previous procedure, we could prepare a list of possible investment outcomes, attach probabilities to their occurrence and write out a separate objective function, expressed as before in terms of the expected disutility derived from the deviations from the desired value of Y.

There is no reason, however, why the range of investment outcomes should be the same as in the case where $\overline{G}$ is used as the policy instrument. A tax change could require forecasters of investment to take into account other features of entrepreneurial behaviour which could suggest a different range of outcomes. Let us assume that the forecasting result is that the range of outcomes is greater. We can then illustrate the comparative position very simply, still using a quadratic objective function of the kind already employed (see Figure IX.2).

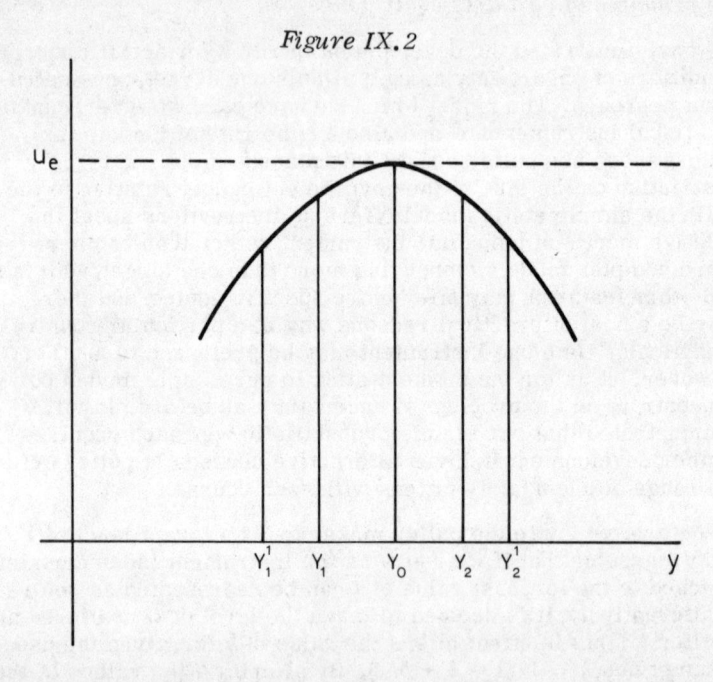

Figure IX.2

In the case in which $\overline{G}$ is used as the policy instrument, we have assumed that there are two investment outcomes, I_1 and I_2, to which probabilities are attached and both of which were associated with the achievement of separate (suboptimal) values for Y, i.e. Y_1 and Y_2 respectively. Similarly, we have identified investment outcomes associated with an alteration in t_y, called I'_1 and

I_2', with which are associated (suboptimal) values of national income, Y_1' and Y_2'. But the difference between the two policy instruments is that in the case of an alteration in t_y the range of investment outcomes is wider.

The problem is: how do we choose between one policy instrument and another? No method of choosing has so far been presented, for nothing has been said about the range of uncertainty. However, common sense suggests that if the range of uncertainty is greater in one case compared with another, this should be taken into account. It is frequently asserted, reasonably enough, that risk aversion should characterize official policy selection.[2] In the particular case under consideration the degree of risk is greater using one instrument rather than another (as measured by the deviations from the optimal level of Y), and it follows that policy makers cannot be indifferent about choosing between them if they are risk-averse. In fact, alterations in G would be preferable to alterations in t_y, for in the latter case there would be a greater risk of, say, unemployment if $Y_1' < Y_1$ and of inflation if $Y_2' > Y_2$.

Given this view of risk, we can proceed to consider how the choice between two instruments designed to achieve the same target can be made and in so doing observe whether or not the certainty equivalence rule applies. We clearly need some measure of the degree of risk associated with the range and probability of alternative outcomes of I, which allows for their multiplier effects on Y. The normal measure adopted is the variance, which is a well-known measure of dispersion about the mean value of a variable, so that a variance term, $\sigma^2{}_y$, is added to the objective function.

Using G as the policy instrument we rewrite the expected utility function as

$$u_e = -\{[Y_0 - k(\overline{I} + \overline{G})]^2 + \sigma^2{}_y\} \qquad (\text{IX. 8})$$

where [3] $\sigma^2{}_y = k^2 \sigma^2{}_I$. Similarly, if it is proposed to use the tax coefficient, t_y, as a policy instrument, and if achieving the desired value of Y thus involved a change in the value of the multiplier rather than a change in the multiplicand, we can express this change in shorthand form as k', i.e. the multiplier value allowing for the desired tax change. Then,

$$u'_e = -\{[Y_0 - k'(\overline{I} + \overline{G})]^2 + \sigma'^2_y\} \qquad (\text{IX. 9})$$

where $\sigma_y'^2 = k'^2 \sigma_I'^2$.

If we maximize these new expected utility functions as found in equations IX. 8 and IX. 9 with respect to G and k' respectively, following the previous procedure after the usual manipulations, we obtain the following expressions:

$$\overline{G} = \frac{Y_0}{k} - \widetilde{I} \qquad (\text{IX. 10})$$

and

$$k' = \frac{Y_0}{\widetilde{I} + G} \qquad (\text{IX. 11})$$

In other words, using each policy instrument singly the principle of certainty equivalence can be invoked. In the absence of consideration of the degree of risk and treating the expected value of I as if it were the certain value, there would be nothing to choose between the use of G and that of k' (i.e. t_y) as a policy instrument. However, if the policy maker were risk-averse there would be a choice. By substituting expression IX. 10 in equation IX. 8, and expression IX. 11 in equation IX. 9, and adopting the certainty equivalence principle so that $\overline{I} = I$, we obtain

$$u_e \gtrless u'_e \text{ as } k^2 \sigma_I^2 \lessgtr k'^2 \sigma_I^2$$

For the policy maker to be indifferent between the two policy instruments clearly requires rather special conditions, given that $k \neq k'$.

III. FURTHER ANALYSIS OF THE STATIC CASE

It would be comforting to think that the problem raised by uncertainty can be dealt with by offering the simple instruction to act according to the principle of certainty equivalence, having regard to the policy makers' attitude to risk, when considering which policy instrument to choose. However, to do this would be to ignore two characteristics of the policy-making situation which introduce fairly drastic modifications into the instruction. The first concerns the shape of the objective function and the second the presence of policy uncertainty.

Let us assume that Y_0 is the desired level of national income because it is the level consistent with a high level of employment without inflation, and that with $Y < Y_0$ there is a lower level of employment also without inflation and with $Y > Y_0$ a higher level of employment but with inflation. The quadratic function $(Y_0 - Y)^2$ describes a situation where equal deviations of Y either side of the (unconstrained) optimum level, Y_0, represent the same loss of utility. However, the policy maker's view of underemployment compared with inflation may not be reflected in this shape of function. It would be quite reasonable to assume, *ceteris paribus*, that if $Y_0 - Y_1 = Y_2 - Y_0$ the policy maker would not be indifferent between Y_1 and Y_2 but would prefer Y_2 to Y_1, his interpretation of the community's wishes being that inflation was preferred to unemployment—assuming, of course, a Phillips-type trade-off existed. The quadratic utility function would then have to be respecified. In a two-dimensional diagram with utility on the vertical axis and Y on the horizontal axis, the negative slope to the right of the coordinate denoting Y_0, i.e. to the right of the maximum, would have to be less steeply drawn than the positive slope to the left.

That the principle of certainty equivalence would not apply in this case should now be obvious, but it may be useful to demonstrate this in a very simple way. Taking the utility function depicted in equation IX.5, then, as $Y_0 - k(I_2 + G) \to 0$, i.e. the utility of Y_2 approaches that of Y_0,

$$\frac{\partial u_e}{\partial G} (= 0) \to k\overline{G}Y_0 - k^2 I_1 + k^2 G^2 \qquad \text{(IX.12)}$$

$$\therefore \quad \overline{G} \to \frac{Y_0}{k} - I_1 \qquad \text{(IX.13)}$$

In other words, the less the loss of utility derived from the investment outcome of I_2, the more the policy maker should act as if I_1 would be the investment outcome. As $I_1 < I_2$, clearly G in equation IX.9 will be greater than G in equation IX.7; i.e. the optimal policy is to choose a value of G higher than the value chosen in the certainty equivalent case.[4]

However, the shape of the utility function is not the only cause which calls for the modification of our previous conclusions, and we now consider the case where, even if we retained the quadratic utility function, the certainty equivalence rule would not be the appropriate one to follow.

So far we have considered uncertainty only in relation to the exogenous variables as reflected in $\bar{I}$, but there may also be uncertainty about the response to policy changes as reflected in the multiplier. Thus in equation IX.1, $\partial Y/\partial G = k$ where the value of k is taken as given, but if response to policy changes is uncertain k may not be known for certain. We take account of this problem first of all in the following way. We assume a single policy objective as before and a single instrument, G. However, k is now regarded as a random variable with variance $\sigma^2{}_k$. To simplify the problem further, we assume that there is no correlation between k and I and that they are thus independent of one another. We now rewrite the objective function to take account of these new assumptions:

$$u_e = -\{[Y_0 - \tilde{k}(\bar{G} + \tilde{I})]^2 + \sigma_y^2\} \qquad (\text{IX}.14)$$

where $\sigma_y^2 = \sigma^2{}_k G^2 + \sigma^2{}_I$.

If we now maximize this function with respect to G as before, we obtain the expression[5]

$$\bar{G}_1 = \frac{\tilde{k}(Y_0 - \tilde{\tilde{kI}})}{\sigma^2{}_k + \tilde{\tilde{k}}^2} \qquad (\text{IX}.15)$$

Thus the assumption of a quadratic utility function, given policy uncertainty, does not lead to the adoption of the certainty equivalence principle. We can go further than this and show that, in 'closing the gap' between Y_0 and $k(\bar{I} + \bar{G})$ in order to optimize, policy action depends on the coefficient of variation of k, i.e. σ_k/k. Rewriting equation IX.10 as $k\bar{G} = Y_0 - kI$ and substituting in equation IX.15 we obtain

$$\bar{G}_1 = \frac{k^2 \bar{G}}{\sigma_k^2 \, k^2} \qquad (\text{X}.15a)$$

We assume equivalence between the mathematical expectation of the value of k in the policy uncertainty case and the certain value of k in the forecasting uncertainty case. Defining $\sigma_k = Vk$ then, by further substitution,

$$\bar{G}_1 = \frac{k^2 \bar{G}}{k^2(1 + V^2)} = \frac{\bar{G}}{1 + V^2} \qquad (\text{IX}.15b)$$

Thus, only if the policy maker is absolutely certain about the value of k, i.e. when $V = 0$, will the 'gap' be fully closed. So long as $V > 0$ then $\overline{G}_1 < \overline{G}$. If we compare the substitution of $\overline{G}_1$ and $\overline{G}$ for G in equation IX. 14, it will be found that the value of u_e will be higher (i.e. the loss of utility will be less) in the case of $\overline{G}_1$, although the reader should not take this on trust but should check through by substitution in equation IX. 14.

One further step can be taken with this analysis of policy uncertainty, which is to demonstrate that the 'standard' result of matching instruments to policies no longer holds, or, put another way, that one should use whatever instruments are available in order to achieve only one target. Within the confines of the simple tools which we have used this point will not be demonstrated in a particularly rigorous way, but a firm indication can be given of the correctness of this conclusion. It is convenient in this extension of the analysis to consider the two instruments government expenditure, G, and lump sum taxes, η, which are part of the 'catch-all' autonomous term $\overline{A}$ in equation II. 2. For simplicity we label this instrument $\overline{A}$, where $A = \alpha - b(\eta - R)$ and $\alpha = 0, R = 0$ and $0 < b < 1$. We further assume that we can ignore $\overline{I}$ and so that

$$Y = k_1 G - k_2 A \tag{IX. 16}$$

We have therefore separate multipliers, k_1 and k_2, associated with each policy instrument. Both are random variables, with variances $\sigma^2_{k_1}$ and $\sigma^2_{k_2}$ respectively.

Following our previous analysis we can now rewrite the welfare function with u_e as the target variable in similar fashion to previous statements:

$$u_e = -\left\{[Y_0 - (k_1 \overline{G} - k_2 \overline{A})]^2 + \sigma^2_y\right\} \tag{IX. 17}$$

where $\sigma^2_y = \sigma^2_{k_1} G^2 + \sigma^2_{k_2} A^2$. Solving as before we have

$$\widetilde{G} = \frac{k_1(Y_0 + k_2 \overline{A})}{\sigma^2_{k_1} + k_1^2} \tag{IX. 18a}$$

and

$$\widetilde{A} = \frac{k_2(k_1 \overline{G} - Y_0)}{\sigma^2_{k_2} + k_2^2}$$

where $\dfrac{\partial u_e}{\partial \widetilde{G}} = 0$ and $\dfrac{\partial u_e}{\partial \widetilde{A}} = 0$. The reader should check for himself that if he invokes the rule for optimization with more than one choice variable or instrument, i.e. $\partial u_e/\partial \widetilde{G} = \partial u_e/\partial \widetilde{A} = 0$, the expression u_e in equation IX.17 is minimized by using *both* instruments. This can be judged to be the case from simple inspection of equation IX.18a, for in this expression $\overline{A}$ (unlike $\overline{I}$ in equation IX.14) is free to be varied by the action of the policy maker.

IV. DYNAMIC CASE WITH STOCHASTIC CONTROL

As we know from the previous chapter, policy makers are indifferent neither to the time it takes to reach a particular target nor to the path by which the target is reached. Our analysis of fiscal policy under conditions of uncertainty only tells us what rules to follow in attempting to minimize the possibility that a given target will not be reached, and it is assumed that, once the appropriate action has been chosen, the target is reached (or deviations from it are minimized) instantaneously. For reasons already made clear in Section V of Chapter VIII we shall not attempt to examine the case of intertemporal maximization, although we should note that the maximization process will be all the more difficult if there is either policy or forecasting uncertainty to be encountered in attempting to follow some optimal path of, say, income or employment. But we can introduce the reader to an associated problem which arises when the object is not only to reach but also to *maintain* a given value of income through time. In this case not only does the policy maker encounter the problems associated with calculating the probabilities to be attached to the values of the exogenous variables, which we have already discussed, but also the nature of the lags in the economic system may, as we have seen in Chapter VI, require him to offset cyclical movements in income.

We confine attention to a simple example employing a stochastic function whose resemblance to the functions used earlier in this chapter will soon be obvious. We write the usual income equation in difference equation form:

$$Y_n = C_n + I_n + G_n \qquad (IX.19)$$

where $C_n = b(Y_n - T_n) + e_n$

$I_n = \overline{I}_n$

$G_n = \overline{G}_{n-1}.$

e_n is a random error or disturbance term representing unpredictable influences (in this case on the level of consumption) such as changes in taste, it being believed that the sum of these influences will behave like a random variable as handled in statistical theory. In this instance we accept the proposition that e_n is an independent variable with zero mean and constant variance, the distribution of the disturbances being left unspecified. The interpretation of government expenditure, G, is that its level is fixed in the previous period (in this particular case example in period $n-1$) and that it is the only lagged variable in the system.[6] So we can rewrite equation IX.19 as

$$Y_n = k\overline{G}_{n-1} + k\overline{I}_n - kb\overline{T}_n + ke_n \qquad \text{(IX. 20)}$$

where $k = 1/(1-b)$ and, as usual, $0 < b < 1$.

Using the familiar quadratic utility function and regarding G_n as the policy variable, the function may be maximized following the previous procedure so that

$$u_e = -\{[Y_0 - k(G_{n-1} + I_n - bT_n)]^2 + \sigma^2{}_y\} \qquad \text{(IX. 21)}$$

where $\sigma^2{}_y = k^2\sigma^2{}_{e_n}$ and

$$\frac{\partial u_e}{\partial G_{n-1}} = 0 = Y_0 - kG_{n-1} - kI_n + kbT_n$$

so that

$$G_{n-1} = G_n = \frac{Y_0}{k} - I_n + bT_n \qquad \text{(IX. 22)}$$

There is no essential difference between this result and that found for the static case in which the certainty equivalence rule can be applied, but it will be noted that it is obtained because the random shock, e_n, is independent of the other variables, so that random shocks in the periods $n-1, n-2 \ldots n-m$ do not affect the value of these variables.

Without requiring a further extension in mathematical complexity we can offer some insight into the problem of stabilizing income when policy makers know enough to be able to assume that there is a lagged element in the random shocks. For example, let us rewrite the consumption function as

$$C_n = b(Y_n - T_n) + b_1 e_{n-1} + e_n$$

where $0 < b_1 < 1$, but retain the other features in the model presented in equation IX. 20. Then maximizing the expanded function IX. 21 with respect to G_n yields the result

$$\overline{G}_{n-1}(=G_n) = \frac{Y_0}{k} - I_n - b_1 e_{n-1} + bT_n \qquad \text{(IX. 22a)}$$

There is one important difference between the control rule depicted in equation IX. 22 and that found in equation IX. 22a, which is that in the latter we have a variable, e_{n-1}, which by its very nature cannot be observed. We have therefore to find a means by which e_{n-1} can be expressed in terms of variables which can be observed. This is obtained in the following way. We substitute equation IX. 22a into the expanded version of equation IX. 20, which now includes the extra term $b_1 e_{n-1}$. We find that

$$e_n = (Y_n - Y_0)/k \qquad \text{(IX. 23)}$$

As this equation holds for every time period,

$$e_{n-1} = (Y_{n-1} - Y_0)/k \qquad \text{(IX. 23a)}$$

which when substituted into equation IX. 22a gives

$$G_{n-1}(=G_n) = \frac{Y_0(1+b_1)}{k} - \frac{b_1 Y_{n-1}}{k} - I_n + bT_n \qquad \text{(IX. 22b)}$$

All this is very well but, even ignoring the fact that the economic models which attempt to show what happens must in reality take a much more expanded form, we are really only on the threshold of a labyrinth of further problems.

As we have already shown earlier in this chapter, devising a rational procedure for achieving the desired linkage between target and instrument(s) does not itself help with the forecasting problem, and the extra element in even our simple model of a lagged random shock emphasizes more than ever the frail nature of the 'evidence' on which policy decisions have to be made and the weighing up of the consequences of wrong forecasting. For example, it can be demonstrated that the deviation of Y from the desired value will be proportionately greater than the deviation of the forecasted value of b_1 from its actual value, even if all other parameters are correctly forecasted. (7) Furthermore, as anyone with an elementary knowledge of modern econometrics will know, we avoided a plague of further difficulties by making all our exogenous variables predetermined, for our random error terms are independent of their past values. If this were not so we could not form a control rule based on variables which can be observed.

V. CONCLUSION

The purpose of this final chapter has been to present an exercise in method rather than to reach any final conclusions about the proper conduct of fiscal policy. Even within its limited scope it may fulfil two kinds of further need beyond the understanding of the simpler analytics of applied macroeconomics. There will be those who may feel that the next stage for them is to study fiscal policy as a set of instruments alongside other instruments of policy, in which case they may find this chapter, and indeed the whole of the latter part of the book, as a point of departure for studying the relative efficiency of budgetary instruments alongside other instruments of policy designed to achieve whatever policy targets are considered relevant. They will soon find that economists have a long way to go in the process of devising optimizing models which contain both a policy-relevant list of objectives and a fully articulated macroeconomic model which can survive the full battery of econometric testing. On the other hand, those with a more specialized interest in public finance will wish to examine more closely the links between what budgetary measures are meant to achieve and how these measures can best be designed, given the problems encountered in employing them in an uncertain world. They will soon find that great ingenuity has often been employed in developing tax and expenditure instruments which, although administratively feasible, may be based on a very crude conception of how the macroeconomic system is meant to work.

As reported in the Coda (Chapter X) to the first edition of this work, the authors have themselves had several opportunities of practising what they preach and offer as a salutary closing lesson the following anecdote.

A few years ago we were involved in a practical study of methods of creating employment by fiscal means in developing countries with rapid rates of population growth. (8) This entailed visiting a wide variety of countries with differing emphasis on and commitment to fiscal policy. In one country visited, the government planning department did not care to use the national accounts officially submitted to international bodies such as the UN and IBRD, which, incidentally, were prepared in the Central Bank. Although there was an official planning committee on which all the major economic ministries and the Central Bank were represented, there was no document published by it which could be taken to embody a set of economic-planning objectives. Whereas detailed study had been made of the effects of the tax system on stability and growth, there was no co-ordination of government expenditure proposals. Different ministries, including the Ministry of Finance, had 'rival' models of the operation of the economy of varying sophistication, which were not necessarily made available to one another. (As one official put it, things are so secret in one ministry that when the daily papers arrive they are believed to be stamped as confidential!) The country concerned had had a decade of a fast rate of growth and relatively stable prices and foreign exchange rate. But over the same period, unemployment had become something of a problem and there had been a definite increase in income inequality.

To the sceptic this confused picture may suggest that, even if some commonly accepted objectives were not attained, the economy in question had achieved much, not despite, but perhaps because of, a political situation which *prevented* policy co-ordination. The enthusiast for economic planning can always answer that one cannot generalize from a sample of one country, and that it is at least conceivable that even in this one instance better articulation of objectives and better policy co-ordination would have produced as good if not better results.

One might resolve this kind of dispute by some kind of cost-benefit study of fiscal planning methods, but this task we must pass over to others. Nevertheless, in taking leave of the reader we must repeat the warning that, whatever technical equipment he may be stimulated to acquire by reading this work, he must not be led to believe that enthusiasm for analysis is necessarily contagious and will take ready hold over those placed in the position of implementing fiscal policy.

NOTES

[1] The *locus classicus* of the discussion of policy formulation under conditions of uncertainty is Henri Theil, *Optimal Decision Rules for*

Government and Industry, North-Holland Publishing Co., Amsterdam, 1964, but this is a rather difficult book. For a useful exposition of simple techniques used in the rest of this chapter see Maurice Peston, *Theory of Macro-Economic Policy*, Philip Alan, 1974, Ch. 6. For applications to government policy see: William Brainard, 'Uncertainty and Effectiveness of Policy', American Economic Association Proceedings, *American Economic Review*, Vol. LVII, No. 2, May 1967; Warren Smith, 'On the Conduct of Monetary Policy' in Smith and Culbertson (eds), *Public Finance and Stabilization Policy: Essays in Honor of Richard A. Musgrave*, North-Holland Publishing Co., Amsterdam, 1974; and Gary Fromm and Paul Taubman, *Public Economic Theory and Policy*, Macmillan, New York, 1973, Ch. 21.

(2) For a defence of this position see G. Fromm and P. Taubman, op. cit., pp. 307-8.

(3) This follows the well-known rule that if every value of a distribution is multiplied by a constant, the variance must be multiplied by the square of the constant. For a formal proof see any good textbook on statistics, e.g. Daniel B. Suits, *Statistics: An Introduction to Quantitative Economic Research*, Murray, London, 1966, pp. 43-9.

(4) Of course, we could reconstruct our utility function by having separate arguments representing deviations from desired levels of unemployment and rate of change of prices (inflation) with each component represented by a quadratic. See M. Peston, op. cit., Ch. 6 Appendix.

(5) See W. Brainard, op. cit., pp. 412-15, and Alan S. Blinder and Robert M. Solow in *The Economics of Public Finance*, Brookings Institution, Washington, 1974, pp. 95-7.

(6) For a useful introduction to simple stochastic systems see Kenneth F. Wallis, *Introductory Econometrics*, Gray-Mills Publishing Company, London, 1972, pp. 14-20 and 38-42.

(7) For exploration of this proposition, and further development of control models embodying budgetary variables, see M. Peston, op. cit., Ch. 9.

(8) The results were distilled in Alan Peacock and G. K. Shaw, *Fiscal Policy and the Employment Problem in Less-Developed Countries*, OECD, Paris, 1971.

Appendix A

SUGGESTIONS FOR ADDITIONAL READING

The following references indicate possible further reading and sources not otherwise indicated in the text.

GENERAL REFERENCES

Auld, D. A. L. 'An Application of Econometrics to Evaluate Fiscal Tax Policy', *Economic Record,* June 1969.

Balopoulos, E. T. *Fiscal Policy Models of the British Economy,* North-Holland Publishing Company, Amsterdam, 1967.

Blinder, A. S. and Solow, R. M. 'Analytical Foundations of Fiscal Policy' in A. S. Blinder, R. M. Solow, G. F. Break, P. O. Steiner and D. Netzer, *The Economics of Public Finance,* Brookings Institution, Washington, 1974.

Brittan, S. *Steering the Economy: The Role of the Treasury,* Penguin Books, Harmondsworth, 2nd edn., 1971.

Brunner, K., Laffer, A. and Okun, A. 'The Political and Economic Aspects of Policymaking: A Symposium', *Journal of Money, Credit and Banking,* Feb. 1972.

Calogero, R. G. D. 'Techniques of Fiscal Analysis in Sweden', *IMF Staff Papers,* July 1974.

Colwell, P. E. and Nash, N. A. 'Comparing Fiscal Indicators', *Review of Economics and Statistics,* Aug. 1973.

Dixon, D. A. 'Techniques of Fiscal Analysis in the Netherlands', *IMF Staff Papers,* Dec. 1972.

Hansen, B. 'On the Effects of Fiscal and Monetary Policy: A Taxonomic Discussion', *American Economic Review,* Sept. 1973.

Hansen, B. (assisted by Snyder, W. W.) *Fiscal Policy in Seven Countries, 1955-65,* OECD, Paris, 1969.

Lewis Jr, W. (ed.) *Budget Concepts for Economic Analysis,* Brookings Institution, Washington, 1968.

Musgrave, R. A. and P. B. 'Fiscal Policy' in R. E. Caves (ed.), *Britain's Economic Prospects,* Brookings Institution, Washington, 1968.

Peacock, A. T. (ed.) *Quantitative Analysis in Public Finance,* Praeger, New York, 1969.
Smyth, D. J. 'The Measurement of Fiscal Performance', *Economic Record,* Dec. 1968.
Snyder, W. W. 'Measuring Economic Stabilisation, 1955-65', *American Economic Review,* Dec. 1968.
Stein, H. *The Fiscal Revolution in America,* University of Chicago Press, Chicago, 1969.
Wand, R. N. 'Monetary and Fiscal Effects on Economic Activity: A Reduced Form Examination of their Relative Importance', *Review of Economics and Statistics,* May 1974.
Worswick, G. D. N. 'Fiscal Policy and Stabilization in Britain', *Journal of Money, Credit and Banking,* Aug. 1969.

CHAPTER II

Bailey, M. J. *National Income and the Price Level,* McGraw-Hill, Maidenhead, 1962.
Barro, R. J. 'Are Government Bonds Net Wealth?', *Journal of Political Economy,* Nov./Dec. 1974.
Cary Brown, E. 'The Static Theory of Automatic Fiscal Stabilization', *Journal of Political Economy,* Oct. 1955.
Christ, C. F. 'A Simple Macro-economic Model with a Government Budget Constraint', *Journal of Political Economy,* Jan./Feb. 1968.
Evans, M. K. 'Reconstruction and Estimation of the Balanced Budget Multiplier', *Review of Economics and Statistics,* Feb. 1969.
Forte, F. and Hochman, H. M. 'Monetary and Fiscal Policy: Ambiguities in Definitions' in Haller and Recktenwald (eds), *Financz- und Geld-Politik im Umbruch,* V, Hase and Koehler, Mainz, 1969.
Hagger, A. 'Multiplier Theory and Fiscal Policy', *Review of Economic Studies,* June 1957.
Haller, H. *Finanzpolitik: Grundlagen und Hauptprobleme,* 4th edn, J. C. B. Mohr (Paul Siebeck), Tübingen, 1968.
Kochin, L. A. 'Are Future Taxes Anticipated by Consumers?', *Journal of Money, Credit and Banking,* Aug. 1974.
Meyer, L. H. 'Wealth Effects and the Effectiveness of Monetary and Fiscal Policies', *Journal of Money, Credit and Banking,* Nov. 1974.
Park, R. E. 'Redistributional Aspects of the Balanced Budget Multiplier: A Comment on the Musgrave, Baumol-Preston

and Hansen Contributions', *Review of Economics and Statistics,* Vol. XLIX, 1967.

Salant, W. 'Taxes, Income Determination, and the Balanced Budget Multiplier', *Review of Economics and Statistics,* May 1957.

Steindl, F. G. 'Money and Income: The View from the Government Budget Restraint', *Journal of Finance,* Sept. 1974.

Zwick, B. 'The Interest-Induced Wealth Effect and the Behaviour of Real and Nominal Interest Rates', *Journal of Finance,* Dec. 1974.

CHAPTER III

Eisner, R. 'Fiscal and Monetary Policy Reconsidered', *American Economic Review,* Dec. 1969.

Hauser, G. and Burrows, P. *The Economics of Unemployment Insurance,* Allen & Unwin, London, 1969, Ch. 4.

Holzman, F. D. and Zellner, A. 'The Foreign-Trade and Balanced Budget Multipliers', *American Economic Review,* Vol. XLVIII, March 1958.

Shaw, G. K. 'European Economic Integration and Stabilization Policy' in Carl S. Shoup (ed.), *Fiscal Harmonization in Common Markets,* Vol. II, Columbia University Press, New York, 1967.

Silber, W.L. 'Fiscal Policy, Tax Structure and the Permanent Income Hypothesis', *Kyklos,* No. 1, 1971.

CHAPTER IV

Auld, D. A. L. 'Wages, Prices and a Progressive Personal Income Tax', *Economic Studies,* Dec. 1970.

Brooman, F. S. *Macro-economics,* Allen & Unwin, London, 1970, pp. 196-200.

Morag, A. *On Taxes and Inflation,* Random House, New York, 1965, esp. Ch. 3.

Peston, M. H. 'The Tax Mix and Effective Demand', *Public Finance,* No. 3, 1971.

Rose, P. S. and Hunt II, L. H. 'The Relative Importance of Monetary and Fiscal Variables in Determining Price Level Movements: A Note', *Journal of Finance,* March 1971.

Williamson, J. 'The Price-Price Spiral', *Yorkshire Bulletin,* May 1967.

CHAPTER V

Cornwall, J. 'The Structure of Fiscal Policy Models', *Quarterly Journal of Economics*, Vol. LXXIX, 1965.
Hall Jr, C. A. *Fiscal Policy for Stable Growth*, Holt, Rinehart & Winston, London, 1960.
Nelson, R. N. 'The Low-Level Equilibrium Population Trap', *American Economic Review*, Dec. 1956.
Peacock, A. T. 'The Public Sector and Economic Growth', *Scottish Journal of Political Economy*, Feb. 1961.
Phelps, E. S. *Fiscal Neutrality Toward Economic Growth*, McGraw-Hill, Maidenhead, 1965.

CHAPTER VI

Auld, D. A. L. 'Automatic Fiscal Stabilizers: Problems of Identification and Measurement', *Public Finance*, No. 4, 1971.
Bailey, M. J. 'The Optimal Full Employment Surplus', *Journal of Political Economy*, July/Aug. 1972.
Baumol, W. J. 'Pitfalls in Contracyclical Policies: Some Tools and Results', *Review of Economics and Statistics*, Feb. 1961.
Brown, E. C., Solow, R. M., Ando, A. and Karaken, J. 'Lags in Fiscal and Monetary Policy' in *Stabilization Policies, Commission on Money and Credit*, Prentice-Hall, London, 1963.
Dixon, D. A. 'The Full Employment Budget Surplus Concept as a Tool of Fiscal Analysis in the United States', *IMF Staff Papers*, March 1973.
Fischer, S. and Cooper, J. P. 'Stabilization Policy and Lags', *Journal of Political Economy*, July/Aug. 1973.
Friedman, M. 'A Monetary and Fiscal Framework for Economic Stability', *American Economic Review*, June 1948.
Morawetz, D. 'Personal Income Taxes and Consumer Spending in the United Kingdom, 1958-1969', *Public Finance*, No. 2, 1973.
Okun, A. M. and Teeters, N. H. 'The Full Employment Surplus Revisited', *The Brookings Papers on Economic Activity*, No. 1, 1970.
Rey, M. *Saggio Sulla Teoria Della Flessibilità Automatica Fiscale*, Guiffré, Milan, 1968. (This volume contains an excellent bibliography on dynamic aspects of fiscal policy.)
Richter, R. and Selten, R. 'Dynamische Theorie der Built-in Flexibility', *Zeitschrift für die gesamte Staatswissenschaft*, 1963.

CHAPTER VII

Artoni, R. 'The Co-ordination of Fiscal and Monetary Policies', *Public Finance*, No. 3, 1970.

Blomqvist, A. G. 'A Note on the Appropriate Use of Monetary and Fiscal Policy under Fixed Exchange Rates', *Swedish Journal of Economics*, Dec. 1970.

Culbertson, J. M. *Macro-economic Theory and Stabilization Policy*, McGraw-Hill, Maidenhead, 1968, Part V.

Dernberg, T. F. 'Exchange Rates and Co-ordinated Stabilization Policy', *Canadian Journal of Economics*, Feb. 1970.

Fleming, J. M. 'Targets and Instruments', *IMF Staff Papers*, Nov. 1968.

Helliwell, J. F. 'Monetary and Fiscal Policies for an Open Economy', *Oxford Economic Papers*, March 1969.

Marrelli, M. 'Policies for Internal and External Stability and Growth', *Public Finance*, No. 4, 1972.

Mundell, R. A. 'Capital Mobility and Stabilization Policy under Fixed and Flexible Exchange Rates', *Canadian Journal of Economics*, Nov. 1963. Reprinted in R. A. Mundell, *International Economics*, Macmillan, New York, 1968, Ch. 18.

Peston, M. H. 'The Correlation between Targets and Instruments', *Economica*, Nov. 1972.

Smith, W. L. 'Monetary-Fiscal Policy and Economic Growth', *Quarterly Journal of Economics*, Feb. 1957.

Takayama, A. 'The Effects of Fiscal and Monetary Policies under Flexible and Fixed Exchange Rates', *Canadian Journal of Economics*, May 1969.

Tower, E. 'Monetary and Fiscal Policy in a World of Capital Mobility: A Respecification', *Review of Economic Studies*, July 1972.

CHAPTER VIII

Fromm, G. and Taubman, P. *Policy Simulations with an Econometric Model*, Brookings Institution, Washington, 1968, Ch. 5.

Hansen, B. *Lectures in Economic Theory: Part II The Theory of Economic Policy and Planning*, Studentlitteratur, Lund, Sweden, 1967.

Morawetz, D. 'Employment Implications of Industrialisation in Developing Countries', *Economic Journal*, Sept. 1974.

Peacock, A. T. and Shaw, G. K. 'Fiscal Measures to Improve Employment in Developing Countries: A Technical Note', *Public Finance*, No. 3, 1971. See also the critique by Banks,

Gulati and Krishman, and Oyejide in *Public Finance*, No. 4, 1972.
Stewart, F. and Streeten, P. 'Conflicts between Output and Employment Objectives in Developing Countries', *Oxford Economic Papers*, July 1971.
Stiglitz, J. E. 'Wage Determination and Unemployment in L.D.C.'s', *Quarterly Journal of Economics*, May 1974.
Theil, H. 'Linear Decision Rules for Macro-Dynamic Policy', in B. Hickman (ed.), *Quantitative Planning of Economic Policy*, Brookings Institution, Washington, 1965.
Tinbergen, J. *Central Planning*, Yale Series in Comparative Economics, Yale University Press, New Haven, 1965.

Appendix B

THE MAIN SYMBOLS USED

AGGREGATES

B	Balance of payments
B^K	Capital account of balance of payments
C	Consumption
C_c	Consumption per capita
C^m	Consumption in monetary units
D	Budget deficit/surplus $= T-G$.
E	Function
G	Government expenditures
G_d	Government defence expenditures
G^m	Government expenditures in monetary units
H	Autonomous element in government expenditure
I	Investment
I^m	Investment in monetary units
I_x	Investment *ex ante*
K	Capital stock
K_c	Capital per capita
K^m	Capital stock in monetary units
L	Total demand for money
L^s	Speculative demand for money
L^t	Transactions demand for money
M	Imports
MS	Money stock
N	Units of employment or labour input
N^a	Average product of labour
NW	Total wages
O	Profits
P	Price or price index
P^c	Price level of consumption goods
P^i	Price level of investment goods
P^k	Price level of capital goods
PQ	Total revenue $=$ Money national income
Q	National output
R	Transfer payments
S	Savings
S_c	Savings per capita
T	Total tax yield
T_i	Indirect taxes

T_y	Income taxes
U	Unemployment
V	Input
V^K	Capital input
V^N	Labour input
W	Total wage
X	Exports
Y	Gross national product/income
Y^c	Capacity income
Y_c	Income per capita
Y^d	Disposable income
Y^F	Full employment income
Y^g	Actual growth of income
Y^m	Money national income
$Y_f{}^m$	Money national income at factor cost
Y^r	Required or equilibrium growth of income
Y^*	Target growth of income
Z	Sum of all autonomous expenditures

CONSTANTS, EXOGENOUSLY DETERMINED PARAMETERS, ETC.

Δ	Increase
Σ	Sum of
Π	Mathematical function
θ	Shift parameter
α	Autonomous consumption—i.e. consumption at zero income
β	Autonomous investment—i.e. investment at zero interest and/or zero income
γ	Speculative demand for money at zero interest rate
∂	Partial derivative
ψ	Exogenous growth rate of population
λ	Lagrange multiplier
η	Taxes at zero income—e.g. lump sum taxes
π	Societies' objective function
σ	Standard deviation
μ	Stabilization or fiscal coefficient
Ω	Accelerator coefficient
ϕ	Incremental capital output ratio
$\left.\begin{array}{l}\epsilon\\\zeta\end{array}\right\}$	Non-defined constants
ρ	Investment ratio

COEFFICIENTS, FUNCTIONAL RELATIONSHIPS, RATIOS, ETC.

b	Marginal propensity to consume
c	Interest-elasticity coefficient of the speculative demand for money
e	Disturbance term
f	Function of
g	Ratio of government expenditures to national income
h	Output-capital ratio
i	Rate of interest
j	Marginal propensity to import
k	Multiplier
k_a	'Domestic' multiplier of country A—i.e. excludes the element of foreign repercussion
l	Commodity l
m	Commodity m
n	Time
p	Percentage of government expenditures of an investment nature
q	Interest-investment coefficient
r	Capital-labour ratio $= K/N$
s	Savings ratio - S/Y
s'	Savings ratio after tax
t_i	Indirect tax rate
t_y	Rate of income tax
u	Utility index
v	Transactions demand for money coefficient
w	Wage rate
$\left.\begin{array}{l}x\\y\\z\end{array}\right\}$	Policy objectives

NOTES

(1) Time derivative $\dfrac{d(\ )}{dn}$ indicated by $(\cdot)$. This $\dfrac{dY}{dn} = \dot{Y}$.

(2) The placing of a bar over a symbol implies that it is being held constant or is autonomously determined. Thus, for example, $\bar{G}$ indicates a constant level of government expenditure.

(3) Subscripts $a, b,$ and n:
Any of the symbols used above may be modified by the use of three commonly employed subscripts. The first two, a and b, define an economic variable, magnitude or coefficient exclusively with respect

to two countries A and B. Thus, for example,
Y_a^d refers to disposable income in country A,
Y_b^d to disposable income in country B.
The subscript n defines the time period concerned. Thus whilst
Y_n^c denotes capacity income at time period n,
Y_{n-2}^c indicates the same concept two periods (years) ago.

(4) Superscripts A and B:
In a like manner the above symbols may be modified by the use of two commonly adopted superscripts A and B. These define a variable specifically with respect to an individual or industry. Hence
V^A = the input of industry A,
u^A = the utility of individual A
and so forth.

INDEX OF NAMES

Ackley, G. 22, 42
Allen, R.G.D. 22
Ando, A. 181
Archibald, G.C. 23, 43
Artoni, R. 182
Auld, D.A.L. 79, 178, 180, 181

Bailey, M.J. 179, 181
Balopoulos, E.T. 178
Barro, R.J. 179
Baumol, W.J. 118, 181
Blinder, A.S. 43, 177, 178
Blomqvist, A.G. 182
Bombach, G. 97
Brainard, W. 177
Brittan, S. 178
Bronfenbrenner, M. 22
Brooman, F.S. 180
Brunner, K. 178
Burrows, P. 65, 180

Calogero, R.G.D. 178
Cary Brown, E. 78, 179, 181
Christ, C.F. 179
Clark, J.B. 63
Cobb, 16, 85, 86, 87, 93, 159
Colwell, P.E. 178
Cooper, J.P. 181
Cooper, R.N. 124
Cornwall, J. 97, 181
Culbertson, J.M. 177, 182

Dernberg, T. 23, 182
Dixon, D.A. 178, 181
Domar, E.D. 11, 16, 80, 81, 82, 84, 86, 93, 97, 109, 144
Dosser, D.G.M. 97
Douglas, P.H. 16, 85, 86, 87, 93, 159

Eisner, R. 180
Evans, M.K. 179

Fleming, J.M. 182
Fischer, S. 181
Forte, F. 179
Friedman, M. 65, 181
Fromm, G. 177, 182

Gelting, J. 29

Haavelmo, T. 29
Hagger, A. 179
Hahn, F.H. 23
Hall, C.A., Jnr 181
Hansen, A.H. 38, 39, 50, 52
Hansen, Bent 23, 127, 128, 143, 178, 182.
Harrod, R.F. 11, 16, 80, 81, 84, 86, 93, 97, 109, 144
Hauser, G. 180
Helliwell, J.F. 182
Hicks, J.R. 11, 38, 39, 50, 52, 118
Hochman, H.M. 179
Holmes, J.M. 65
Holzman, F.D. 22, 180
Hunt II, L.H. 180

Johansen, L. 22
Johnson, H.G. 97

Kaldor, N. 11
Kalecki, M. 11
Karaken, J. 181
Keynes, J.M. 15, 25, 36, 37
Kilpatrick, R.W. 6, 65
Kochin, A. 179

Laffer, A. 178
Lagrange, L. 91, 141, 145, 156
Laidler, D.E.W. 65
Lefeber, L. 159
Lewis, W., Jnr 178
Lipsey, R.G. 23, 43

Marelli, M. 182
Matthews, R.C.O. 22
McDougall, D.M. 22
Meyer, L.H. 179
Miller, M.H. 117
Morag, A. 180
Morawetz, D. 181, 182
Mundell, R.A. 129, 132, 135, 136, 182
Musgrave, P. 178
Musgrave, R.A. 22, 78, 97, 117, 178

Nash, N.A. 178
Nelson, R.N. 181

Okun, A. 178
Ott, D.J. 124
Ott, A.F. 124
Park, R.E. 179
Patinkin, D. 22
Peacock, A.T. 43, 79, 97, 117, 118, 177, 179, 181, 182
Peston, M.H. 177, 180, 182
Phelps, E.S. 181
Phillips, A.W. 139, 140, 142, 143, 169
Pigou, A.C. 40

Rey, M. 181
Richter, R. 181
Rose, P.S. 180

Salant, W. 180
Samuelson, P.A. 11, 18, 106, 118
Sato, K. 97, 98
Sato, R. 97

Selten, R. 181
Shaw, G, K. 136, 177, 180, 182
Shoup, C.S. 22
Silber, W. 65, 180
Smith, W.L. 177, 182
Smyth, D.J. 65, 97, 108, 118, 179
Snyder, W.W. 179
Solow, R.M. 11, 43, 97, 177
Stein, H. 179
Steindl, F.G. 180
Stern, R.M. 65
Stewart, F. 183
Stiglitz, J.E. 183
Streeten, P. 183
Suits, D.B. 177
Sumner, M.T. 65

Takayama, A. 182
Tanzi, V. 119
Taubman, P. 177, 182
Teeters, N.H. 181
Theil, H. 19, 21, 23, 177, 183
Tinbergen, J. 19, 21, 23, 127, 128, 183
Tower, E. 182

Wallis, K.F. 177
Wand, R.N. 179
Williamson, J. 79, 180
Worswick, G.D.N. 179
Wrightsman, D. 65

Zellner, A. 180
Zwick, B. 180

INDEX OF SUBJECTS

Accelerator 62-4, 103, 110 *see also* Multiplier-Accelerator
Aggregate supply function 16, 150
Automatic monetary stability 39-42
Automatic stabilization 32-36, 108-14
Automatic stabilizers versus discretionary Policy 100-2, 116-17

Balance of trade effect of income expansion 48
Balanced budget multiplier 28-32, 45, 83, 123
Built-in flexibility 102, 108, 116; and economic growth 109-14; distinguished from automatic stabilization 102

Certainty equivalence, principle of 162f
Cobb-Douglas production function 85-9, 159
Consumption function 25, 27, 54, 59, 62
Consumption Tax 69; versus income tax as stabilizer 70f
Cost-Push inflation 76-7

Debt Finance 40-2, 58-60
Developing Countries: and employment creation 148f; and Keynesian policies 149-54

Employment multiplier 68, 142
European Economic Community 64

Fiscal 'Drag' 114, 116
Fiscal policy: and constrained maximization Chapter VIII; and economic growth 81f; and employment 68, 139-43, 148f; and intertemporal utility maximization 157-9; and neo-classical growth theory 84f; and non-linear models 120f; and technical change 93-5; and the price level 70f, 139f; and the theory of economic policy 19-21; and uncertainty Chapter IX; in a dynamic setting 102f, 172-7.
Full employment budget surplus 114f
Full employment objective 14, 139, 143

'Golden Age' solution 80, 84, 93
Government expenditure multiplier 28f
Government Transfers Multiplier 30f

Hansen-Tinbergen approach to economic policy 19, 21, 127, 128
Harrod-Domar growth model 81f, 109f, 144
Hicks-Hansen IS/LM analysis 38f, 54, 58f.

Incomes policy 143
Input-output table 152
Interest Rates: and international capital movements 50; and investment 37f, 62, 121; and the balance of payments 49, 50f

Keynesian:
Analysis of Fiscal Policy 11f; Expenditure Model 24f; Fiscal Policy Model, Deficiencies of 13f; Model, Extension of 36; Policies, Applicability to Developing countries 148

Lagrange Multiplier 136, 141, 145

Mathematics: contents of this volume 21-2; List of symbols Appendix B; Money and national income 36f
Money supply, exogenous determination of 38, 123
Monetary sector 36f, 49f, 59, 60
Multiplier-accelerator analysis 63, 103f
Mundellian model 129f

Neo-classical growth theory 84f

Objective function 15, 19, 128, 131, 139, 144, 155; and constrained maximization 137f; quadratic 164, 169, 170, 171, 173

Permanent income hypothesis 54f; effect on expenditure multiplier of 57
Phillips Curve, 140f
Post-Keynesian developments in macro-economic theory 12f, 54f
Premium Bonds 43

Production Function 26, 68, 86, 153
Profit Maximization 66, 69

Random shocks 173-4

Social welfare function *see* objective function
Stochastic control 172f
Stabilization policy: and dynamics 100f; destabilizing consequences of 101, 107, 114, 116

Tax harmonization 65
Tax multiplier 33, 35
Theil Approach to Economic Policy 19, 21, 127, 177
Time: and Economic Stability 17f, Chapter VI; and inter-temporal utility maximization 157f; Tinbergen approach to economic policy 19, 21, 127; 'trade-off' problem 18f; two-country model 44f

Uncertainty: forecasting 162; policy 162, 170
Utility function, shape of 169
Wage-price spiral 76-7
Wealth Effects 58f